The Triumph of Meanness

THE TRIUMPH
OF MEANNESS

America's War Against
Its Better Self

NICOLAUS MILLS

HOUGHTON MIFFLIN COMPANY

BOSTON   NEW YORK   1997

For information about this and other Houghton Mifflin trade and reference
books and multimedia products, visit The Bookstore at Houghton Mifflin
on the World Wide Web at http://www.hmco.com/trade.

Library of Congress Cataloging-in-Publication Data
Mills, Nicolaus.
    The triumph of meanness : America's war against its
better self / Nicolaus Mills.
        p.   cm.
    Includes bibliographical references and index.
    ISBN 0-395-82296-3
    1. United States — Civilization — 1970–   2. United States —
Social conditions — 1980–   I. Title.
    E169.12.M545   1997
    973.92 — dc21   97-3389   CIP

Printed in the United States of America

QUM 10 9 8 7 6 5 4 3 2 1

FOR KATHIE BARNES APTER

AND IN MEMORY OF

CESAR CHAVEZ AND FRED ROSS

ACKNOWLEDGMENTS

I owe a special debt to my researchers, Kelly Braffet, Dina Pancoast, Julianne Rana, Dylan Siegler, and David Yaffe. Ken Barkin, Fawaz Gerges, Mark Levinson, Brian Morton, Ross Miller, Ray Seidelman, John Seidman, Michael Walzer, Sean Wilentz, and my editor, Steve Fraser, provided me with readings that saved my bacon time and again. Sarah Lawrence College gave me time off and freedom in the form of a Hewlett-Mellon Fellowship and a Julie and Ruediger Flik Travel Grant, and the Sarah Lawrence College librarians proved once more that what makes a research library great is not the size of its holdings but the ingenuity of its librarians.

Contents

The Triumph of Meanness

Introduction

AT A SUBWAY STOP near where I live in New York, the city has recently taken out most of the old wooden benches and installed new pop-up plastic seats that return to a vertical position the minute you stand up. Compared with the old benches, the seats are small and uncomfortable. They are so narrow that the best you can do is balance on them by leaning forward, as if you were a jockey riding a horse. For the city, however, the seats are a great plus. It is impossible for homeless people to sleep on them. They are, to use an expression coined by urban sociologist Mike Davis, "bumproof."[1]

The idea of bumproof benches and seats isn't new. But our acceptance of them as the norm for our cities is. In New York they are consistent with Mayor Rudolph Giuliani's "quality of life" strategy for keeping beggars and the homeless out of the subway stations at all costs, and for the country as a whole, they reflect a much broader trend in which meanness — large and small — has become our first response to a series of social problems that we face.[2]

Any number of journalists have reported on the new meanness. Looking into just the top folder on my desk, I find a *New York Times* column, "The Politics of Meanness," by Anna Quindlen; an unsigned editorial with the same title in the *Christian Science Monitor*; an op ed by Neal Gabler entitled "A Multitude of Meanness" in the *Los Angeles Times*; and a *Washington Post* essay by Judy Mann, "The Cost of the Politics of Meanness." For me such articles have proved invaluable. What is important to see, I believe, is that in the 1990s meanness is not just a political response we make periodically in our weaker moments. Meanness today is a state of mind, the product of a culture of spite and cruelty that has had an enormous impact on us. We have all too quickly adapted to the thinking embodied in pop-up subway seats to deal with our long-term problems.[3]

In his 1972 bestseller, *The Mountain People*, anthropologist Colin Turnbull created a sensation with his account of the Ik, an East African tribe whose customs and economy had been destroyed by the development going on around them. In reaction the Ik fashioned a culture that devalued everything from the family to ordinary kindness. "The Ik have successfully abandoned useless appendages, by which I refer to those 'basic' qualities such as family, cooperative sociality, belief, love, hope, and so forth," Turnbull wrote, "for the very good reason that in their context these militated against survival." Self-interest alone, Turnbull went on to say, shaped the world of the Ik. We are far from being the Ik. But it is in their direction that our meanness is taking us, I believe, and it is crucial to see how this process is happening if we want to put a halt to it.[4]

"We will never regard any faithful, law-abiding group within our borders as superfluous," Franklin Roosevelt observed in his Second Inaugural Address. "The test of progress is not whether we add more to the abundance of those who have much, it is whether we provide enough for those who have too little." Sixty years after Roosevelt's Second Inaugural, that egalitarian test is still, I think, the best measure of our progress and humanity, and at the core of *The Triumph of Meanness* is the contention that as a nation we are failing that test. The income gap between the richest Americans and everyone else is, according to a 1996 Census Bureau report, now wider than at any time since the end of World War II, and the worst part is, we don't care. The culture of meanness has hardened us to the suffering of the very poor. Typical is California's affluent Orange County, which went bankrupt in 1994 after its treasurer made a series of disastrous investments in the bond market, losing $1.7 billion. By 1995 Orange County was in the midst of belt tightening, but it was not the middle class or the affluent who were most affected. As a county supervisor acknowledged, "It's been the disadvantaged and the poor and the incarcerated who have felt what this bankruptcy is about." Their services, from staffing at the local welfare agency to a homeless outreach program, were the ones the county cut rather than approve a proposed half-cent increase in the sales tax that would have brought in $800 million.[5]

In this respect Orange County is America in micro-cosm. But it is more than just a war on the poor that the culture of meanness has made possible. What has been go-ing on simultaneously over the course of the 1990s is a "third worldization" of the country, in which only those at the top have real security. At Sarah Lawrence College, where I teach, we now have a scholarship category for stu-dents with "newly revealed need." What it acknowledges, albeit with a euphemism, is a terrifying fact of middle-class life in the nineties: job loss for the forty-five- to fifty-five-year-old businessman or woman who, having reached what was once a secure place in management, is suddenly sacked for a younger, cheaper worker as a company down-sizes. Since 1970 the middle class, those making between $20,000 and $75,000 a year, has shrunk from 57 percent to 47 percent of the population, but in the business atmo-sphere that is part of the new culture of meanness, they get little sympathy. As an AT&T executive observed after the company announced in 1996 that it was laying off 40,000 employees, workers need to think of themselves as self-employed vendors rather than as company men or women who can expect a secure future.[6]

It is not, however, only those who are directly victim-ized by the culture of meanness and the new rules it has le-gitimized who are trapped by it. All too often, so are those who try to combat the new meanness and the inequities it imposes. In 1991 in Pennsylvania, Harris Wofford, a former associate director of the Peace Corps and ex-president of Bryn Mawr College, won a special election to the Senate by campaigning for health-care reform against Richard Thornburgh, a former attorney general in the Bush administration and before that a popular Pennsylvania governor. What was significant in the special election was Wofford's health-care strategy. Instead of arguing that a poor or middle-class family should have the same rights to certain basic services as a wealthy one, Wofford took the opposite line to make the same point. "If criminals have the right to a lawyer," Wofford told voters, "I think working Americans should have the right to see a doctor." It was a strategy that left Thornburgh without a comeback. But it also showed how the culture of meanness has affected us. Only by using spite and envy, by taking the contempt the average voter feels for a criminal and turning it on its head, could Wofford make the case for humane social legislation.[7]

If I had been living in Pennsylvania in 1991, I would have voted for Wofford. But what he had to do to win is frightening, and it is the implications of such mean options that I think we need to scrutinize. In the long run they don't offer the building blocks for a decent society. Far easier and far more typical in the 1990s is attacking the rights of a criminal or the poor in a way calculated to bring everyone down a peg.

▪   ▪   ▪

"With the cold war over but millennium jitters upon us, new bad guys are required," *New York Times* columnist Maureen Dowd recently observed of our current obsession with scapegoating and villainizing. That's not a bad shorthand account of the historical forces that have shaped the culture of meanness. It just doesn't go far enough. The end of the Cold War has given us enough of a sense of security to see our prime enemies as internal, but we have not gone around picking bad guys randomly in order to make ourselves feel good. There has been a real pecking order at work. Large businesses, having found that they can hire foreign workers more cheaply than American workers, complain that their employees don't work as hard as they should and that they have failed to retrain themselves for the new economy. Middle-class workers, in turn, join with business in treating the inner-city poor as if they were strangers from foreign nations whose habits and values put them beyond the reach of help. Nearly six out of ten whites in a 1995 survey said they would not pay more in taxes to increase spending on poor minorities, but even more telling is the statement by a self-employed businesswoman and ex–Vista volunteer who in describing the political anger she was feeling observed, "I can't afford to support illegitimate babies, women who have five abortions, and poor people who don't want to work."[8]

The results of this new social pecking order with its harsh stereotyping of the poor have most often been described in terms of our division into two nations: the first well-off and mostly white; the second poor and mostly black and brown. But I think this view fails to give the full picture. What has really been lost over the course of the 1990s is the idea of nationhood. We simply write off, find superfluous, to use the language of Roosevelt's Second Inaugural, whole segments of the population. The negative side of this meanness is easy to see. More prisons. More police. Less welfare. Decaying public schools. But the positive side of the same equation is just as revealing. It is fortress America with gated suburbs and guarded apartment houses and private schools and private security forces.

For an increasing percentage of the country, the obligations of nationhood have turned into a burden, and what the culture of meanness has supplied is the justification for those who feel this way to shed their connection with everyone but people like themselves. Where all this is taking us in terms of the end of the idea of nationhood may be seen in the defense of large-scale immigration (the *Wall Street Journal* has called for open borders) that is now popular in many business circles. Typical is California businessman Ron Unz, a Republican challenger to Governor Pete Wilson. In defense of the notion of taking in more immigrants, Unz writes, "In Los Angeles the vast majority of hotel and restaurant employees are hardworking Hispanic immigrants, most here illegally, and anyone who believes that these unpleasant jobs would otherwise be filled either by native-born blacks or whites is living in a fantasy world. . . . The only means of making a job as a restaurant busboy even remotely attractive to a native-born American would be to raise the wage to $10 or $12 per hour, at which level the job would cease to exist — this is Economics 101."[9]

If one doesn't examine this statement very closely, Unz seems to be defending an updated version of Emma Lazarus's famous Statue of Liberty poem in praise of our welcoming the world's huddled masses and wretched refuse. But in fact, what Unz is actually championing is the idea of an American urban peasantry, a servant class that works cheaply and efficiently and doesn't require benefits. He does not care whether these urban peasants ever become citizens, nor does he worry about their impact on those who need ten- and twelve-dollar-an-hour jobs to support themselves and their families. Unz's America — and increasingly ours as a consequence of the culture of meanness — is a country without shared hopes and obligations. It is no accident that during the summer of 1996, when previews for the sci-fi thriller *Independence Day* began running in theaters across the nation, the film's most publicized scene, the blowing up of the White House by space aliens, drew loud cheers from audiences rather than, as the movie's producers expected, gasps of horror. We have become suspicious of the whole notion of the government, symbolized by the White House, acting for the common good.

▪ ▪ ▪

If historical precedents are any guide, I think that changing course will take much longer than we imagine. Since the end of World War II, our most generous times, those eras when we acted as though we were a single people, have come when we felt sure about our prosperity and unthreatened by the prospect of sharing. The GI Bill, the Peace Corps, the War on Poverty, Medicare, and Medicaid all came when we were feeling flush.

These days we sense that our modern Golden Age, which began in 1945 and ended in the early 1970s, will not return. We know we cannot recapture the kind of prosperity that came from once supplying 40 percent of the world's output, and our instinct in a time of downward mobility is to hold on to our share of what we see as a diminishing economic pie. If in the future we become a more generous and cohesive society, it will have to be on the basis of an ethic of comparative scarcity. We will have to believe that because there is less to go around than in the past, we need to be all the more committed to sharing what we do have. The Puritans of the early seventeenth century and the New Dealers of the 1930s were successful in making the case for such an ethic of sharing. Our problem is that it is not an ethic with which we have been comfortable over the last half century.[10]

Which isn't to say that we cannot change. It is simply that doing so will be an uphill battle. What gives us the best chance for change is, I believe, coming to terms with the no-win position in which the culture of meanness has put us, and for this reason the chapters that comprise this book are essentially descriptive rather than prescriptive in their focus. I think it is essential for me to try to put in perspective a series of widely reported events — black church burnings in the South, a Riverside, California, sheriffs' assault on illegal immigrants, the 1995 Oklahoma City bombing — that we know about but don't necessarily link together. But just as important to keep in mind, I believe, are those aspects of the culture of meanness that show up in our daily lives in more routine ways and reveal what we are entertained by or prepared to tolerate. I don't think we can afford to ignore the popularity of pay-per-view television programs that feature bare-knuckle fighting. Nor, by the same token, can we just dismiss as bad taste what in 1996 became the newest craze in Dallas: a twenty-five-dollar tour of the route of President Kennedy's fatal motorcade that ended with a race to the hospital where he died.[11]

In emphasizing this cultural mix, I am not suggesting that all meanness is the same. A corporation that pays its CEO millions while brutally downsizing is different from a middle-class worker who, feeling pinched, wants to see welfare payments cut, and a fan of ultimate fighting, as the new bare-knuckle brawls are called, is different from a frightened middle-class worker. But what all of them help to further is a culture in which cruelty wins out over compassion and "civic empathy," to use journalist Michael Tomasky's term, loses its power. Meanness in any one area — institutional, social, or personal — makes meanness in every other area easier to achieve.[12]

In an essay ironically titled "Down with Compassion," the social critic Ellen Willis pointed out the dangers of overmoralizing about this trend. "If the welfare state is in deep trouble, the reason is not that people are somehow meaner than they used to be but, rather, that economic and social conditions have changed," she observed. Willis was right to remind us that over the course of the 1990s our basic human nature has not changed. But that does not mitigate the degree to which our thinking and behavior have become different — that is, meaner — and in so doing made us increasingly willing to be harder on others if we think the results will benefit us.[13]

In his 1996 book *Who Owns the West?* the Montana essayist William Kittredge wrote of his own feelings about contemporary America, "Many of us live with a sense that there is something deeply and fundamentally wrong in our society. Many of us feel our culture has lost track of the reasons one thing is more significant than another. We are fearful and driven to forget the most basic generosities." The uneasiness Kittredge describes is rooted in bad conscience, and to me it seems the right response to the culture of meanness that surrounds us and that we have allowed to get out of hand. Having a bad conscience doesn't by itself guarantee that we will change, but it is a starting point and one that I hope *The Triumph of Meanness* will provide the grounds for cultivating.[14]

PART ONE
More Than a Right Turn

1   Mean Times

As THE 1990s DRAW to a close, it is clear that we are not the same country we were when the decade began. There is a meanness in our public and private lives that has changed the way we see ourselves and the future. Like the bumper stickers that ask "Where is Lee Harvey Oswald when his country needs him?" we have crossed a line that not long ago seemed to mark the outer bounds of decency.[1]

Meanness — as a politics of spite and cruelty that targets the vulnerable — is not new in American life. In the past it has been used to defend everything from Indian removal to immigration quotas. More recently it has been the basis of whole political careers. During the Great Depression Father Charles E. Coughlin gained national prominence when he combined his criticism of the Roosevelt administration with attacks on Jewish international bankers. In the 1950s Senator Joseph McCarthy achieved even greater power by creating a red scare that panicked the country and cost thousands of innocent people their jobs, and in the 1960s Governor George Wallace became a national figure when, in a dramatic showdown with the Kennedy administration, he challenged the right of blacks to enroll in the University of Alabama.[2]

In the long run Coughlin, McCarthy, and Wallace could not withstand the test of public scrutiny; decency triumphed over the political meanness they embodied. But the meanness of the 1990s, which is as much cultural as political, is an altogether different matter. Like the old meanness, it surfaces in the savaging of an opponent or in an appeal to hidden fears that makes it easy to scapegoat a person or group. The vindictiveness of the new meanness was impossible to miss in the first weeks of the 104th Congress, when the openly gay Democrat Barney Frank was called "Barney Fag" by Dick Armey, the Republican House majority leader, and more recently the new meanness has surfaced in the South, where a wave of black church burnings has revived memories of the Jim Crow past. But in contrast to the old meanness, which tended to be directed at distinct and limited targets, what characterizes the new meanness is that its spite and cruelty have become pervasive. They are part of our everyday world in ways that we now take for granted.[3]

The new meanness is not just reflected in a political shift to the right that sends welfare back to the states for the first time since the New Deal and says we should cut Head Start while adding billions more to the defense budget than the military requested. The new meanness is also style and attitude, meanness without guilt, as one critic of it observed. We see the new meanness in a combativeness in which the president's opponents insist that he is "the enemy of normal Americans" and a senator warns him that he "better have a bodyguard" if he enters the senator's state. We hear it on talk radio when G. Gordon Liddy advises his listeners on the best way to shoot a federal agent. We read about it after law enforcement officials raid a California sweatshop in which foreign workers were kept under guard around the clock and paid fifty cents an hour for the sewing they did. We observe it in professional sports, where veteran basketball coach Pat Riley fines his players for helping an opponent up from the court.[4]

Fed up with the political meanness he saw dominating Congress, Maine's moderate Republican senator, William Cohen, announced in early 1996 that he would not run for a fourth term, and two weeks later, in a *Washington Post* op ed, he explained that what bothered him most was the worsening partisan atmosphere in Congress, with debate overshadowed by "an increase in personal hostilities" that allowed "rhetorical finger-pointing" to replace civility. The other side of the coin is, however, that rather than let meanness get to us, as Cohen, currently secretary of defense did, we have over the course of the nineties come to accept it, even enjoy it. On television the success of a prime-time series like *Melrose Place*, where the key to high ratings is a predatory sexual war among the young and the beautiful, is no isolated case. Meanness has also become central on the afternoon talk shows, where a middlebrow host like Phil Donahue can no longer make it; the field has been flooded with shows like those of Jerry Springer and Jenny Jones, in which the formula for success is to turn the guests against each other in humiliating tell-all battles. Even the news-format programs have not been immune from using meanness to win a following. CNN's *Crossfire* pits panelists against each other in a war of political put-downs, and *The McLaughlin Group* and *Capital Gang* follow a similar pattern. Most significant, what works for the mass audience of television works in other areas as well. Rap has cultivated a huge audience with music in which women are regularly described as "hos" and "bitches," and in sports, taunting an opponent and showing him up after a score has become a routine strategy for heightening tension and involving fans in the game.[5]

The pervasiveness of the new meanness is reflected in the Lexis-Nexis database system. In 1980 the system had only 115 entries on the subject of meanness. By 1985 the number of entries was 171. But by 1990 the number had more than doubled to 498, and by 1995 the number had more than tripled to 1,883. What makes our current culture of meanness so dangerous, however, is that it represents more than a spontaneous souring of our national disposition or a renewal of what historian Richard Hofstadter called the paranoid style in American politics. These days the new meanness has, as sociologist Murray Hausknecht notes, reached the point where it is institutionalized. We find it easier and easier to think the worst

of each other and, as the assault on the safety-net programs of the 1930s and 1960s shows, to live in a society
that has little room for generosity or empathy.[6]

Central to the new meanness, as well as distinguishing
it from the confident Reaganism of the 1980s, is our feeling
that we are no longer a coherent nation bound together by
our past. In the espionage films of the 1990s, such as *Under
Siege* and *Broken Arrow*, the enemy is not the agent of a
foreign country but an American, a former CIA or military
man now willing to sell to the highest bidder the very
weapons he once guarded. He has no qualms about being
loyal to his own interests above all others, and neither do
we. The security that in the past we derived from a Cold
War that defined our enemies, an economy that offered
each generation a brighter future, and a civil rights movement that gave us moral purpose, is gone, replaced by the
belief that it no longer makes sense to act as if we shared
the same fate or could find common cause. Our best option, we now imagine, is to save ourselves and those like us
on the basis of a lifeboat ethics that rewards ruthlessness.

■　■　■

At the core of the new meanness lies the vacuum created
by the fall of the Berlin Wall in 1989 and the collapse of
the Soviet Union. For the first time since the start of the
Cold War, we are without a superpower that threatens our
survival or an ideological rival whose social system requires constant comparison with ours. The result has been
an opportunity, seemingly boundless in its possibilities,

for turning inward. But what has happened instead is that in turning inward we have for a variety of reasons come to apply the language and thinking we once used on our Cold War enemies to ourselves. For the right, the new enemy has become the inner city and liberalism. For the left, burdened in the past with the charge of being soft on communism, the new liability has become being soft on crime and welfare.

That the nineties would be a decade in which domestic concerns replaced foreign concerns was signaled by George Bush in his 1992 State of the Union Address, when he declared that, with the Cold War over, America could at last begin to act in ways that were impossible when its avowed enemy was a superpower. "Now we can look homeward even more, and move to set right what needs to be set right," Bush announced in a speech that called for lower withholding taxes, economic deregulation, and an attack on a welfare dependence that was "passed from generation to generation like a legacy."[7]

It was not, however, George Bush, but Pat Buchanan at the Republican National Convention of 1992 who defined the harshness with which the inner Cold War of the 1990s would be waged. In a speech entitled "The Election Is about Who We Are: Taking Back the Country," Buchanan argued that a religious war was being waged for the soul of the country. "It is a cultural war as critical to the kind of nation we shall be as the Cold War itself," he explained. This cultural war was being fought, he said, between those who play by the rules and those who don't, and he brought his speech to its conclusion and his audience to its feet by asserting that the Los Angeles riots of 1992 epitomized the new cultural battlefield and its winnability for conservatives. For Buchanan the heroes of Los Angeles were the troops "who had come to save the city," and in his closing paragraph he paralleled their actions with those America needed to take to restore its cultural greatness. "As those boys took back the streets of Los Angeles, block by block," Buchanan told the convention, "we must take back our cities, and take back our culture, and take back our country."[8]

Buchanan's speech, filled with references to the Democrats as pro-gay and pro-lesbian, was immediately attacked by the media for its sexual bigotry, and his broader cultural critique got lost in the controversy. But by 1993 the ideas that Buchanan had voiced at the Republican National Convention had achieved mainstream respectability. In his 1993 essay "My Cold War," the conservative critic Irving Kristol gave them intellectual foundation. "Now that the other 'Cold War' is over, the real cold war has begun," Kristol wrote. "It is a far more interesting cold war — intellectually interesting, spiritually interesting — than the war we have recently won," he declared, "and I rather envy those young enough for the opportunities they will have to participate in it." Kristol considered it crucial that those who believed in the old Cold War should volunteer for the inner Cold War that lay ahead.[9]

The new alien philosophy, as dangerous to our way of life as Communism had once been, was, as far as Kristol and an increasingly conservative segment of the electorate were concerned, now identified as liberalism. And the new enemy, as dangerous as the old Soviet Union, was now seen as those people living within our midst — most often in big-city slums — whose values and lifestyles made them the equivalent of an alien nation. "We have to cut off the head of the enemy, and the enemy is the homeless," the New York City police captain charged with rousting the homeless from Central Park in the summer of 1994 told reporters shortly after beginning his task. In liberal New York the captain's remarks brought intense criticism, but in the country as a whole, the mood was very different. Years earlier, in an article entitled "The Liberals' Legacy of Failure," Newt Gingrich had argued, "There are a hundred potential Beiruts in America today, and we are in danger of losing control of entire neighborhoods." By the 1994 congressional campaign Gingrich could expand his Beirut analogy into a far broader coded message about the inner Cold War the country needed to wage. In speech after speech Gingrich won over audiences and helped produce a Republican majority in the House and Senate for the first time in forty years by insisting "It is impossible to maintain civilization with twelve-year-olds having babies, fifteen-year-olds killing each other, seventeen-year-olds dying of AIDS, and eighteen-year-olds receiving diplomas they cannot read." Gingrich could count on a middle-class electorate that was sympathetic to his message and prepared to believe the worst of people they saw as "others." He could also count on that electorate having heard much rougher political language on talk radio. For the nationally syndicated talk-show host Rush Limbaugh, welfare recipients were the "dependency class," and for New York's Bob Grant the city's black mayor, David Dinkins, was "the men's room attendant."[10]

What has made this middle-class electorate so willing, as *Harper's* magazine editor Lewis Lapham put it, to blur the distinctions between race and politics and moral behavior is its own bitter experience of downward mobility. In contrast to the years from 1947 to 1973, when average weekly earnings grew by 60 percent, recent decades have been hard on most families. Since 1989 the typical American household has seen its annual income fall by 7 percent, and among white-collar workers the shock has been particularly great. In 1993 for the first time in history, white-collar unemployment was higher than blue-collar unemployment. Workers who earn $50,000 or more a year now account for twice as many lost jobs as they did in the 1980s. As the Economic Policy Institute observed, "Having a college degree no longer affords protection against falling wage trends."[11]

To make matters worse, the usual cures for job loss and falling wages have not worked in the 1990s. Although corporate profitability is at a thirty-year high and productivity has risen by 24 percent since 1979, companies continue to downsize by shedding workers who are close to retirement, slashing benefits, and cutting wages. The result has been the kind of jobless prosperity that reverses the philosophy of "Engine Charlie" Wilson, head of

General Motors in the 1950s, who in the company's heyday popularized the slogan "What's good for General Motors is good for the country." In the 1990s the use of cheap foreign labor and the elimination of managerial jobs through computerization have made American companies more competitive but have also severed the links between profit, productivity, and middle-class security. Charlie Wilson's General Motors, now a much smaller company than it was in the 1950s, has been doing its best to outsource jobs and bypass its well-paid workforce. The business stars of the nineties are represented by CEOs like "Chainsaw Al" Dunlap, who during his two-year tenure at Scott Paper earned his reputation and nickname by firing 11,000 workers in the belief that the "responsibility of the CEO is to deliver shareholder value. Period."[12]

The consequence has been a growing disparity between the incomes of CEOs and everyone else's pay. In 1974 the typical American CEO made 35 times the average worker's pay. By the nineties it was 150 times, compared to a 16 to 1 ratio in Japan and a 21 to 1 ratio in Germany. And in big companies, often the ratio didn't tell the full story. In 1995, in seventy-six of the nation's one hundred and fifty largest companies, the median salary and cash bonus for chief executives topped $2 million.[13]

Small wonder then that we have a nervous workplace, in which all employees, except top management, see themselves as disposable, even when they do everything that is asked of them. In a 1993 speech to the Council on Institutional Investors, Secretary of Labor Robert Reich described this change in terms of a broken contract. "There used to be an unwritten contract between top managers and workers. If you made a good effort to do your job, you could count on having that job as long as the firm stayed in business," Reich observed. "But that implicit contract is being abandoned at an ever faster pace. Even reasonably healthy companies are cutting their payroll." The old middle class, Reich contends, has become the new anxious class.[14]

The anxiety of the workplace Reich describes is the basis of cartoonist Scott Adam's nationally syndicated comic strip *Dilbert*, which focuses on the trials of a computer operator trying to survive in a large office where firings and insecurity are part of the air he breathes. Dilbert, whose boss tells him that employees are our ninth most valuable asset (carbon paper is eighth), manages to get by through humor and indifference. He does not succumb to a world in which, as far as he is concerned, humiliation is a management tool.[15]

But in political terms much more than quiet suffering defines the new anxious classes. In contrast to the workers of the 1930s, who believed that solidarity was in their interest, today's workers, especially those who regard themselves as middle class, have no such confidence. Aware of the ease with which they can be replaced, they simply try to get by on their own. The new anxious class has, as a consequence, also become the new angry class, venting its frustrations on those who seem to be getting a free ride on welfare or through affirmative action preferences. In the

1993 film *Falling Down*, Michael Douglas, playing a laid-off missile-plant worker known only by his vanity license plate, D-Fens, portrayed the politics of this anger in a long and bitter rampage in which D-Fens's first targets were a Korean store owner and a group of Latino gangbangers. Although angry with his employers, D-Fens's instinct is not to go after them. He has no belief that the corporate world he once depended on can be changed. Like the anxious class, he prefers to target the "outsiders" he sees spoiling a society he once felt comfortable in.[16]

In any era the anger of a middle class worried over its declining fortunes would make for a politics of resentment. In the 1990s, however, middle-class and working-class anger has been pushed to new levels with the unprecedented rise of negative political campaigning. As Stephen Ansolabehere and Shanto Iyengar note in *Going Negative*, their 1995 study of political advertising, "A decade ago attack advertisements were just a small fraction of the messages aired by candidates. Now, politicians come out swinging. By the most comprehensive accountings, fully half of all political commercials emphasize the weaknesses of opposing candidates rather than the strengths of the sponsors."[17]

Negative political campaigning is not, to be sure, new. The Federalist press insisted that Thomas Jefferson was having relations with his slave Sally Hemmings. Abraham Lincoln was called an ape, buffoo, coward, drunk, Negro, savage, robber, and traitor, and in the notorious election of 1888, President Cleveland was charged both with beating his wife and appointing brothelkeepers to office. But the modern negative campaign, which puts so much emphasis on savaging a candidate and what he stands for, is different in kind from those of the past.[18]

Its incivility, although often shaped by the values of a candidate, is impersonal, arising from a television technology that has made the thirty-second sound bite the primary form of politicking and given media consultants enormous power. These days the most effective political ads, as demonstrated by the Willie Horton commercial of 1988, which linked Democratic presidential candidate Michael Dukakis to the crimes of a black convict he furloughed while governor of Massachusetts, combine a suggestive visual with a brief negative message and, in the words of historian Wilson Carey McWilliams, make the innuendo concrete. It is virtually impossible to answer such negative ads with the brevity or effectiveness of the original ad.[19]

Michael Dukakis would have had to answer the Horton ad by showing that his prison furlough program was similar to that of both the Republican governor before him and those of most states in the country. Then he would have had to argue that Horton's violation of his furlough was the exception in a program that was more than 95 percent effective. Dukakis was not unique in facing such an uphill battle, nor was the Bush campaign exceptional for taking advantage of his situation. As former Democratic congressional whip Tony Coelho observed during the 1994 midterm elections, "The only way you can win races today is with negative ads."[20]

Coelho's cynicism is borne out by the response of voters to negative ads. As Ansolabehere and Iyengar show, the majority give greater weight to negative information than to positive information when forming their judgments of a candidate, and in general elections a negative ad will on average give its sponsor a boost of nearly ten points over a positive version of the same ad. What is more, a politician who on principle wants to run a wholly positive campaign puts himself at a disadvantage. Voters expect a candidate who is attacked to respond with a negative ad. If he refuses and responds only with a positive ad, they see him as flawed and unwilling to defend himself. The moral is very clear. Given the likelihood that any campaign will turn negative, the best strategy is to strike first and put your opponent on the defensive. For Republicans, moreover, there is a bonus; as the party opposed to big government, they are able to use attack ads far more successfully than Democrats in appealing to their supporters and to independents, since both groups are basically skeptical of government and politicians and thus find negative ads highly credible.[21]

In terms of the politics of meanness, the result has been the blending of technology and social sensibility. Whether one wants to stigmatize a whole group (AFDC mothers as welfare queens) or trash an individual (civil rights attorney Lani Guinier as quota queen), it has become easier and easier to do so. There is, moreover, no end in sight for where negative campaigning will stop. The most vicious television ad in the 1996 congressional elections occurred in California, where Republican Tom LeFever morphed the face of Richard Allen Davis, the killer of Polly Klaas, into that of Democratic incumbent Vic Fazio, but for the most part, the new negative campaign has made far more sophisticated use of technology. Push polling — a process by which workers for a candidate call up voters and, in the guise of conducting a legitimate survey, spread rumors about their candidate's opponent — has become widespread in the nineties, and at the same time technology has also made negative campaigning cheaper. Opposition research on a rival's financial and personal life, once labor intensive and time consuming, has become comparatively inexpensive thanks to the computer, and so has negative-persuasion telephoning, which with computer-aided dialing allows a single operator to make eighty to one hundred calls an hour at a price of forty-five cents to a dollar thirty per call.[22]

Standing for a very different kind of politics not too many years ago would have been a civil rights movement that by example showed it was possible for America to change moral course. But in the 1990s the civil rights movement has not simply disappeared from sight. It has been subsumed by the belief that in the wake of the Reaganism of the 1980s and the lost affirmative action battles that have followed, interracial alliances are out of the question and that it is futile to argue for social justice on the basis of a broad universalism.

How remote even the memory of the civil rights movement has become for a large segment of the black community was reflected in the summer of 1994 when Rosa Parks was mugged in the living room of her West Side home in Detroit by a young black man, who beat her and stole fifty-three dollars. Neither Mrs. Parks's age nor her status as the woman whose defiance of the Jim Crow laws of Alabama began the Montgomery bus boycott of 1955–56 was enough to ensure her safety in her own neighborhood.[23]

A year later in a very self-conscious way, the Million Man March of 1995 set out to invoke and then bury memory of both the March on Washington of 1963 and the civil rights movement. Superbly organized by the Nation of Islam and drawing heavily on working-class and middle-class blacks, the Million Man March made a point of not only excluding women and all whites but centering on Louis Farrakhan. "The attempt to separate the message from the messenger is not going to work," the Reverend Benjamin Chavis, the national director of the march, warned. The result was a march that, in contrast to the 1963 March on Washington, which helped pave the way for the Civil Rights Act of 1964, wound up, as Jesse Jackson later complained, "essentially disconnected" from national politics. But more than that, it was a march that, by virtue of Farrakhan's well-known anti-Semitism and conspiracy theories, made it easy for critics to dismiss black demands for social change as no longer part of an agenda that represented the moral high ground. Indeed,

Farrakhan himself seemed to want to court hate, releasing on the Friday before the march an interview in which he again called Jews "bloodsuckers" and then compounded his attack with the assertion that in recent years Arabs, Koreans, and Vietnamese had been coming into the black community as merchants and also behaving like bloodsuckers.[24]

■ ■ ■

What in turn has emerged in the 1990s in the absence of a civil rights movement capable of claiming the moral high ground is a new self-righteousness that asserts American society is basically fair as it now stands and that those at the bottom of society are there because they deserve to be.

The genetic version of this argument surfaced in 1994 in Charles Murray's and the late Richard Herrnstein's *The Bell Curve*, which used differences in IQ scores to explain the way in which poverty in America follows racial lines. For Murray and Herrnstein, the standard deviation between blacks and whites (sixteen points) provided a logical explanation for income differences in a society in which the marketplace puts a heavy premium on intelligence, and rather than being seen as offering up what Harvard biologist Stephen Jay Gould called an "anachronistic social Darwinism," their book quickly became a bestseller, providing a public anxious for a reason to cut social programs with grounds for arguing that there is a good scientific explanation why blacks in particular cannot be helped by more welfare.[25]

But what has made the new self-righteousness so broadly appealing to an angry and worried white electorate is that it has not relied on anything as predetermined as IQ. It has rested instead on the idea that failings in character and initiative, rather than inheritance, class, or racism explain who is poor. Nobody has done more to popularize this view than William Bennett, the former Reagan secretary of education and Bush drug czar. The author of the bestseller *The Book of Virtues*, Bennett has been relentless in linking the moral decay of the "criminogenic" inner city and its "super-predators" with the moral decay of America. "Current trends in out-of-wedlock births, crime, drug use, family decomposition, and educational decline, as well as a host of other social pathologies, are incompatible with the continuation of American society as we know it. If these things continue, the republic as we know it will cease to be," Bennett has warned. As the decade has progressed, such thinking has gained more and more proponents. It is a short step from Bennett's belief that "illegitimacy is America's most serious problem and welfare is illegitimacy's life support system" to the ideas of Robert Rector, the conservative policy analyst for the Heritage Foundation, who insists, "There are five behaviors that characterize the underclass: out-of-wedlock births, eroded work ethic, criminal behavior, low educational aspirations, and drug use."[26]

For the very wealthy, what is so comforting about this view is that it justifies what the late Christopher Lasch in *The Revolt of the Elites* called their decision to leave the poor behind by sending their children to private schools, moving to isolated suburbs, and protecting themselves with hired security guards. But for middle-class voters worried about their own downward mobility, such thinking is also welcome. There is, it says, no need for them to feel responsible for, let alone guilty about, the misery of the poor, since the source of their problems is not a declining job base but "behavioral poverty." As Robert Rector put it in an interview with the *Wall Street Journal*, "One of the truly stupid ideas of the twentieth century is that if you give people indoor plumbing, free housing, free food, they'll stop killing each other."[27]

The Contract with America relied on such thinking to justify its call for massive cuts in the poverty programs of the New Deal and the Great Society, and nowhere were the Contract supporters' assumptions about behavioral poverty more clearly on display than in the 1995 debates over welfare in the House of Representatives. Time and again the supporters of the Contract raised the fear that the poor have developed an animal-like dependency on welfare. During the debates Florida Republican John L. Mica held up a sign that said "Don't Feed the Alligators" in order to draw an analogy between the measures his state was taking to keep its alligators from becoming overly dependent on handouts and the measures Congress needed to take to control welfare. Republican Barbara Cubin of Wyoming offered a similar analogy — but one that overtly suggested a predatory society should be our model — with her account of what had happened to the wolves in her state. Having been fed elk and venison by the Forest Service, the wolves had, she noted, lost their desire to hunt on their own.[28]

The harshest features of the Contract with America were defeated in 1995 and 1996 because of presidential vetoes and voters' worry that such middle-class entitlements as Medicare and Social Security would be reduced. But what has not gone away is the idea that the poor, especially those from the inner city, must be watched over and disciplined. While espousing fiscal austerity, liberals and conservatives alike have had no qualms about expanding traditional institutions of confinement and using them to send a message.

The classic case was Newt Gingrich's proposal to put the children of poor, underage single mothers in Boys Town–style orphanages. The high yearly cost of the orphanages — as much as $48,000 per child, compared with the $15,000 the average single mother with two children gets in benefits — killed Gingrich's proposal when critics did the arithmetic and found that it could cost $40 billion a year. But the spirit behind Gingrich's plan has not died. There has been renewed faith in the 1990s that prisons and capital punishment are worth every penny.[29]

In 1994 the combined federal, state, and local expenditure for prison construction and maintenance was $30 billion (AFDC at the time was estimated at $25 billion), and since then financially pressed state legislatures have made punishment more publicly theatrical and vengeful than at any time since the 1950s. In 1995 Alabama reintroduced chain gangs, dropping them only after a successful suit by the Southern Poverty Law Center. Mississippi brought back its traditional striped prison uniforms, and New York, at an estimated future cost of $118 million per year, legalized the death penalty.[30]

Left behind as a relic of the past has been the idea of social compassion. In many ways it was an easy target, given the government-bashing of the last two decades and people's doubts about the effectiveness of social programs. Even before the end of the Clinton administration's first year, a *Washington Post*–ABC News poll revealed that 56 percent of those asked believed the nation's problems were so great that "no president could do much to solve them." In the same survey 52 percent said they would rather spend a week in jail than serve four years in the White House. What the culture of meanness has done with such doubts is allow them to be seen as virtues and in turn a justification for compassion fatigue. As David Frum, the conservative author of *Dead Right*, shrewdly noted during a symposium on the future of Republicanism, "People are tired of the constant moaning they hear about the poor. A lot of middle-class taxpayers feel that they're paying more and more for the poor and that the poor are behaving worse and worse."[31]

The results speak for themselves, not only in terms of welfare but in terms of a broader assault on compassion that has become part of the 1990s. As long as a program can be attacked as welfare-like, it becomes vulnerable, as Republican House Majority Leader Dick Armey showed in 1993 when he went after AmeriCorps, the Clinton administration's national service proposal, as a "welfare program for aspiring yuppies." In this atmosphere it has become the norm for fewer of us to work as volunteers for an organization like the Red Cross and for most of us — 77 percent — to bypass the panhandlers we see on the street. By contrast, what comes with increasing frequency is the kind of impatience that prompted the widely respected *New Yorker* dance critic Arlene Croce to complain in a 1995 review that she and audiences were now being imposed upon by a victim's art that required them to feel sorry for "dissed blacks, abused women, or disfranchised homosexuals."[32]

■ ■ ■

Even the counterculture of the nineties has not provided a consistent alternative to the meanness of the mainstream culture. In the 1960s "Make love, not war!" became the rallying cry of Vietnam War protestors, but these days the counterculture has been anything but gentle. The charming hit men of Quentin Tarantino's *Pulp Fiction* talk hiply of the existential choices in their lives, but in their love of the good life, in their willingness to be ruthless for a price, they are morally indistinguishable from the people they kill.

The same attitude thrives in the real world of the nineties. From the relatives of mass murderer Jeffrey Dahmer's victims proposing to raise money for themselves by auctioning the tools he used for torture and cannibalism to the supporters of Lorena Bobbitt triumphantly making snipping motions with their fingers after her acquittal for cutting off her husband's penis, the counterculture has proved as harsh and cruel as mainstream culture. The shock of the April 19, 1995, bombing of the Federal Building in Oklahoma City initially came from the carnage it produced, but as time has passed, what has shocked us more is our discovery that the two men accused of the crime were not simply crazed bombers nor, as originally thought, foreign terrorists. They were part of an organized militia culture, estimated to number as many as 40,000, that views the government as the enemy and has organized itself across the country, stockpiling weapons, threatening federal officials and neighbors, and convening its own courts.[33]

In the face of a culture and counterculture that offer such grim alternatives, what remains is the feeling that anything goes. It is as though we had been given the license to indulge ourselves in ways that would have seemed taboo a short while ago. In our cities underground dog fighting and cock fighting have gained a new foothold, and on pay-per-view television, extreme fighting, in which the combatants slug it out in bare-knuckle brawls held in a steel cage, draws audiences that pay in the millions to watch. Even the law has not escaped the new meanness. The show trials of the decade — those of O. J. Simpson, Susan Smith, Erik and Lyle Menendez — were quickly turned into revenge spectacles by the way they were covered and reported. What they offered viewers was not courtroom insight so much as the pleasure of seeing the tables turned and those accused of murder made vulnerable themselves. Suddenly exposed were O. J. Simpson's wife beating, Susan Smith's thoughts on drowning her children, the Menendez brothers' anger over being forced to have homosexual relations with their father.[34]

A decade ago, during Ronald Reagan's second term, historian Arthur Schlesinger, Jr., confidently predicted, "At some point shortly before or after 1990, there should come a sharp change in the national mood and direction — a change comparable to those bursts of innovation and reform that followed the accessions to office of Theodore Roosevelt in 1901, Franklin Roosevelt in 1933, and of John Kennedy in 1961." Such a change, whether one thinks of it as a new reform movement or, as a number of journalists have, a neo-Progressivism, is not, it is now apparent, going to be happening any time soon, and nothing finally makes that clearer than the nostalgia for shame that has become part of nineties culture.[35]

We would be better off if we could rediscover the sense of shame that the Victorians made so central to British culture, the conservative historian Gertrude Himmelfarb argues. It would allow us to stigmatize illegitimacy as "wrong and shameful," she insists. The same benefits, Marvin Olasky contends in his 1992 study, *The Tragedy of American Compassion*, would follow from stigmatizing welfare for all but the most needy. We went wrong, he argues, with the decision we made with the Great Society programs of the 1960s "to uncouple welfare from shame."

For Newt Gingrich, an admirer of both Himmelfarb and Olasky, each is right, and in *To Renew America* he goes out of his way to point up that since becoming speaker of the House, one of his best-received speeches was one he delivered extemporaneously at the National League of Cities in which he declared, "It is shameful to be a public drunk at three in the afternoon. . . . It is shameful for males to have children they refuse to support. . . . It is shameful for radio stations to play songs that advocate raping and mutilating women." Even Colin Powell, who rarely sermonizes, observes in his recent autobiography *My American Journey* that one reason he thought about entering politics was that "we seem to have lost our sense of shame as a society."[36]

In the 1990s the Republican party has, however, no monopoly on the nostalgia for shame. Communitarian Amitai Etzioni supports dunce caps for schoolyard trouble-makers ("More humane than jail") and believes that it is better to "err on the side of self-righteousness" in our present situation. Liberal *Nation* and *Vanity Fair* columnist Christopher Hitchens, writing on "The Death of Shame," bemoans the fact that we have become a "shameless people," unwilling to accept responsibility, and in 1993 one of Bill Clinton's most successful speeches was one in which, speaking in the church where Martin Luther King delivered his last sermon, he imagined King returning and his listeners feeling shame as he told them, "I fought to stop white people from being so filled with hate that they would wreak violence on black people. I did not fight for the right of black people to murder other black people with reckless abandon."[37]

What lies behind this nostalgia for shame is the sensibility anthropologist Ruth Benedict described more than fifty years ago in *The Chrysanthemeum and the Sword* when she drew a distinction between shame cultures, which rely on external sanctions and the loss of face to regulate behavior, and guilt cultures, which rely on internalized feelings of right and wrong to achieve order. In the 1990s our nostalgia for shame, our wish to inflict it on others, carries with it the implicit admission by the right and the left that there is no longer a point in appealing to what lies deepest inside us.[38]

It could be worse, we tell ourselves. We take comfort in the fact that we now have federal legislation that prevents health maintenance organizations from forcing new mothers and their infants to leave the hospital twenty-four hours after delivery, and we are encouraged that there has been a media backlash against CEOs who receive huge end-of-the-year bonuses as they downsize their companies. But the solace we find in such victories is an indication of how much meanness has defined life in the nineties. In the end its triumph comes not in the defeat of all other considerations but in our willingness to settle for less, to put aside our better selves. We celebrate the disasters we have staved off rather than look forward to a future that is an improvement over the past, and we take for granted, as we show by not voting in record numbers, that elections cannot cure what is most wrong.[39]

2 The New Savagery

On March 25, 1995, agents of the American Society for the Prevention of Cruelty to Animals staged the largest raid in the organization's history. Aided by thirty New York City police, a dozen ASPCA agents swooped down on a converted movie theater in the Bronx and broke up an event billed as the National Championship Cockfight.[1]

The national championship claim may have been hyperbole, but what the ASPCA agents found when they entered the theater was no local cockfight for neighborhood aficionados. The raid, which received front-page coverage in the *New York Times*, provided a startling portrait of a secret world in which promoters stood to earn as much as $30,000 in admission fees, betting, and illegal sales of food and alcohol. The converted Bronx theater where the cockfight was held contained a fighting pit and bleachers, along with false walls designed to be pulled together in case of a raid. Outside the theater cameras and lookout guards provided security. Inside, an area nearly the size of a football field held parking spaces for the 289 spectators, who had paid twenty dollars each for admission.

The ASPCA agents found twenty birds already dead from the night's fighting and ninety more locked in cages. The ninety birds, too violent to be turned loose on a farm, all had to be destroyed. Crossbred with pheasants for aggressiveness, given steroids to build their muscles, and injected with PCP, or angel dust, to deaden the pain of fighting, the birds — each valued between $1,000 and $10,000 — were unfit to do anything but kill each other.[2]

The ASPCA's March raid brought to 1,600 the number of fighting roosters it had seized in New York over the past twelve months and in the revelations it provided offered an eerie reminder of the nineteenth-century New York City described by Luc Sante in *Low Life*, his history of old New York. Sante notes that in 1875 admission to dogfights and cockfights ran as high as two dollars but that the real moneymaker was rat baiting, in which a fox terrier was put in a pit filled with rats and bets were made on how many rats the terrier could kill in a half hour. So far rat baiting hasn't made a comeback, but along with cockfighting, dog fighting has.[3]

At organized dogfighting matches, for which the dog owners sign contracts, up to $500,000 may be bet in a single weekend of fighting, and in inner cities across the country, informal matches have become routine. In the nation's capital the number of dogs animal control authorities have had to put down as a result of fighting has more than tripled over the last five years. The dogs, pit bulls bred for strength and aggressiveness, are turned loose in matches in which money, drugs, cars, or simply social status are the prize. A dog with a good record in fighting can even be an investment. Pit bull pups now sell for as much as $500.[4]

What is happening in the animal world is not, however, an isolated occurrence. Very much part of nineties culture is the rise of a new savagery in which violence is chic and the winner-take-all ethic of the economy has become part of sports and entertainment. When the violence or threat of violence is camp — as in the current S & M club scene or in the sex play of Madonna's videos — it is easy to take or leave. But for the most part there is nothing innocent about the new savagery and its influence.[5]

For martial arts fans, the latest entertainment is extreme fighting or ultimate fighting, which in the form of pay-per-view television extravaganzas like the Ultimate Fighting Championships has drawn 250,000 viewers and grossed $3.4 million in a single evening. In opposing an extreme fighting match that was scheduled for New York City, State Senator Roy Goodman described it as "human cockfighting." It is easy to see why. Although the sport has been likened by its promoters to a celebration of our natural urges, what is most striking about it is the way it has been sold as the next best thing to a fight to the death. As the announcer tells the audience before the fights begin, "This is real, it's live, it's brutal."[6]

The creative director of ultimate fighting is John Milius, the film director of *Conan the Barbarian*, and the presentation of the Ultimate Fighting Championship captures the Conan aesthetic and then some. In place of traditional ropes, the ring in which the fighters battle is surrounded by a wire-mesh fence that cages them in and emphasizes the idea that no escape is possible. Hair pulling, butting, kneeing in the groin — everything except biting and eye gouging — is allowed. In the earliest Ultimate Fighting Championships even the referee was not allowed to stop a fight if it became too one-sided. So far nobody has been killed, but the fights, in which the contestants wear neither gloves nor protective equipment, are predictably bloody. A fighter can be hit while lying on the canvas, and since there are no rounds, the damage from a single fight can be enormous. For both losers and winners, the hospital is often the next stop after a bout.[7]

To date the gender line has not been crossed in ultimate fighting, but the taboo that has kept women out of the most violent sports in the past has, as the appearance of women's boxing champ Christy Martin on the cover of *Sports Illustrated* shows, all but evaporated in the nineties. In 1995, for the first time in history, women entered New York's Golden Gloves Boxing Tournament, and in the more brutal sport of kickboxing, women have become featured performers, quickly adapting to the violence of the ring. "I caught her with a looping right hook to the back of her head and whoomp, down she went. Her mind said get up, but her legs said for what?" Fredia Gibbs, women's super-lightweight kickboxing champion of the world, told reporters after winning her title before 10,000 fans at the San Jose Arena in California.[8]

■   ■   ■

"It was a mistake to think them harmless curiosity seekers. They were savage and bitter," Nathanael West writes of the crowd that riots at the end of his Great Depression novella *The Day of the Locust*. West's description of a crowd taking out its frustrations in violence speaks to the traditional notion of savage pleasures as an outlet for the deprived. But in the 1990s the new savagery is not simply the reflection of an underclass frustrated by hard times. It is also part of a middle-class culture that in recent years has seemed more and more at home with violence.[9]

Even the very young are not exempted from the new savagery, as the popularity of True Crime cards shows. Although True Crime cards have not replaced sports cards in the $2 billion-a-year trading card industry, they have made substantial inroads, with more than 8 million sold in a single year. The appeal of the cards, which come in a foil-covered pack that features a shadowy picture of a criminal against a background of blood spatters, is in the information they offer on gore and violence. Although the True Crime cards include famous crime fighters like the FBI's Elliot Ness and J. Edgar Hoover, the big sellers are the serial murderers, Jeffrey Dahmer, Ted Bundy, Charlie Manson, and "Son of Sam" killer David Berkowitz. What the kids get for their money is a grim photo and a bio telling just what the killer did before he was caught — in Dahmer's case, got his victims drunk, then "photographed, strangled, and dismembered" them.[10]

The most telling sign of the inroads the new savagery has made among kids is, however, reflected in video games. In video arcades across the country, the hottest game in the nineties has been Mortal Kombat, which features characters vying for the title of the world's toughest street fighter. The figures in Mortal Kombat, which look more like photographs than cartoons, don't just hit each other. They throw punches that send animated blood flying, tear out a still-beating heart, and in one case rip off an opponent's head and hold it up, with the spinal cord dangling from the neck.[11]

The home versions of Mortal Kombat are milder, but for kids who have had their appetite for violence whetted by viewing the original in arcades, there is still plenty of gore. In 1994, 6 million Mortal Kombat video games were sold, and in stores like Toys "R" Us the game has become a standard item. It has also been the source of spinoffs and imitators. There has been a *Mortal Kombat* movie and Mortal Kombat Live Tour, and in video arcades across the country, variations on the theme range from Narc, in which a player tries to kill as many drug dealers as possible, to Operation Thunderbolt, where the target of choice is Middle Eastern terrorists.[12]

For those interested in the savage pleasures, it is not, however, necessary to come up with the thirty-five- to seventy-five-dollar price of a game like Mortal Kombat.

Television is doing its best to make ersatz combat a regular feature. *American Gladiators,* a syndicated weekly show that features men and women competing in contests ranging from Joust (a battle with pugil sticks on a platform twenty feet above the ground) to Breakthrough and Conquer (a combination of football and sumo wrestling), has become a major hit as a result of its ability to persuade viewers that they are watching an updated version of the arena games of old Rome. In contrast to *Roller Derby* in the 1950s or today's *Wrestlemania,* the games on *American Gladiators* are for real. Pitted against the regular gladiators, who bear such names as Ice, Nitro, Lace, and Gemini, are contenders who get on the program by competing in tryouts. Viewers not only get a chance to root for their favorite gladiator, they get a weekend athlete's fantasy of imagining how they would do as contestants.[13]

Most significant of all for television and the new savagery is, however, the transformation that has taken daytime talk shows from conversation to confrontation. In 1995 Jonathan Schmitz, a contestant on the *Jenny Jones Show,* shot another contestant, Scott Amedure, when the show was over. The reason for the shooting was that on the program Amedure confessed that he had a crush on Schmitz and wanted to tie him up and spray whipped cream and champagne on his body. Schmitz had expected that the surprise guest with a crush on him would be a woman and felt utterly humiliated at the idea of being thought gay.[14]

No one could have predicted that Schmitz would react

as he did, but it is not surprising that the new talk television has become such a source of violence. As the former producer of the *Jane Whitney Show* told *TV Guide*, "When you're booking guests, you're thinking, 'How much confrontation can this person provide me?'" In contrast to the traditional talk shows of Maury Povich and Oprah Winfrey, on which guests often reveal aspects of their personal life that are controversial or painful, the new confrontational shows pit guests against one another. In the words of Martin Berman, the executive producer of *Geraldo*, "For a show on rape, it used to be enough to interview the victim. Now you need the victim and the perpetrator. You need her to come face to face with her rapist."[15]

The *Geraldo* formula is one that applies to virtually any talk-show situation and works by setting the guests against each other from the start or creating an ambush by having one or more guests held offstage, where they cannot hear or see the show, then having other guests say derogatory things about them on camera. The result in both cases is a show that ultimately revolves around the guests baiting each other. Normally the baiting stops short of physical violence, but violence is always in the air, and by design the show's winner is invariably the guest who can put everyone else in the worst light.

If there is an end in sight for our nineties love affair with the new savagery, it is hard to see. A century ago prizefighting was outlawed in a majority of the then forty-four states. Every time a highly publicized bout was announced, clergymen rushed to deliver sermons denouncing it. Today's equivalents of those sermons are political press conferences, and as conducted by senators John McCain of Arizona and Ben Nighthorse Campbell of Colorado, they have forced the Ultimate Fighting Championships to change cities. But on the whole, political opposition to the savage pleasures has been scattered and ineffective. In 1995 Senate Majority Leader Bob Dole made headlines when he charged that Hollywood and the record industry had brought us to a point "where our popular culture threatens to undermine our character as a nation." At the same time that he was attacking cultural violence, however, Dole was opposing a ban on assault weapons, and the party he led was yielding to pressure from the National Rifle Association and voting down legislation outlawing "cop killer" bullets, which can pierce the protective vests worn by police.[16]

Dole's contradictions are hardly unique. If anything dominates the 1990s focus on law and order, it is the brutality it has sanctioned. On the fringes is the vigilantism of a group like Dead Serious, an anticrime organization in Dallas, Texas, that promises its members a $5,000 cash reward if they kill someone while being robbed or attacked. But much more serious is the kind of thinking that has made us willing, in the midst of cries for smaller government and lower taxes, to spend an estimated $30 billion a year on prison construction and maintenance. What we want for our prison dollars these days is conspicuous punishment that doesn't just put criminals away but humiliates them and, when possible, takes their lives. So much the better if the world we are reminded of is that of the Warner Brothers 1932 film hit *I am a Fugitive from a Chain Gang*. The key, in the words of Charles Crist, the Republican state senator who sponsored the bill authorizing chain gangs in Florida, is for criminals to be treated with a "visible and obvious" harshness. In 1995 Alabama responded to the call for harshness by reintroducing the chain gang and going out of its way, until a suit by the Southern Poverty Law Center forced the state to ban chain gangs as cruel and unusual punishment, to make sure those on the gangs were seen doing roadside work. Mississippi brought back its old green-and-white striped prison uniforms, and in state after state legislators have made a point of showing how willing they are to take an eye for an eye by reinstituting the death penalty. In 1995 there were more executions, fifty-six, than in any year since 1957, and 3,054 inmates were on death rows.[17]

■ ■ ■

To make matters worse, since the decade began, even the counterculture has played a role in the rise of the new savagery. In contrast to the sixties counterculture, with its emphasis on social protest and dropping out of the mainstream lifestyle, the nineties counterculture has accommodated itself to the notion of an eye for an eye.

Militia groups, now estimated by the Treasury Department to have as many as 40,000 members nationwide, are increasingly willing to confront the government and to celebrate what sociologist James William Gibson calls "warrior dreams." The 1995 bombing of the Oklahoma City federal building, with its chief suspects' links to militia groups in Michigan and Arizona, may be an aberration, but the militia culture's ties to the violence and the government conspiracy theories that made that bombing possible are not an aberration. In the militia culture of the nineties, festivals like Gunstock '95 have become the equivalent of Woodstock, and best-selling reading has become a novel like William Pierce's *The Turner Diaries*, which recounts a militia war fought between 1989 and 1999, that peaks with the blowing up of the FBI's computer complex in Washington with a fertilizer bomb.[18]

But the biggest change in the nineties counterculture has been on the left, where groups and individuals that have traditionally been the victims of violence now revel in the new savagery. In 1994, when battered wife Lorena Bobbitt was put on trial for cutting off her husband's penis after what she claimed was a night of sexual abuse, she immediately received the support of feminists across the country. Any notion that Lorena Bobbitt's actions had to be seen in perspective vanished. Outside the courthouse her supporters sold buttons that read "Lorena Bobbitt for Surgeon General" and T-shirts with the logo "Love Hurts." By the time she was acquitted, those who sided with her saw her not as a desperate woman brutally reacting to a brutal marriage but as a triumphant symbol of female rage, a wife who did to her husband what more women ought to do. In the end it was hard to tell the difference between Bobbitt jokes — "Hey, she just threw it out, it's not like she put it in a Cuisinart," the comedian Joy Behar quipped — and the commentary of a serious feminist like Barbara Ehrenreich, who in a *Time* magazine essay slyly observed, "If a fellow insists on using his penis as a weapon, I say, one way or another, he ought to be swiftly disarmed."[19]

It is, however, in pop music that the counterculture has done the most in recent years to legitimize the new savagery. Among white rock bands with large followings, Guns N' Roses has long been notorious for its hate lyrics. Its breakthrough hate record, "One in a Million," came out just as the 1980s were ending and made a point of targeting blacks, gays, and immigrants.

"Don't need to buy none of your gold chains today," Guns N' Roses declared in lyrics that then went on to assert that "immigrants and faggots" were ruining the country by spreading disease and treating America as if it were a mini-Iran. The viciousness of "One in a Million" didn't faze Guns N' Roses fans, and by the early 1990s their record "Pretty Tied Up" was adding to their bad-boy reputation with lyrics about a "bitch" who craved abuse from all the band members:

> She ain't satisfied without some pain
> Friday night is going up insider her — again

Even the normally mild Michael Jackson hasn't been above allowing an unmistakable viciousness to creep into his records over the course of the nineties. Before he decided to change the words, two million copies of his hit "They Don't Care about Us" were released with lyrics in which the anti-Semitic rhymes — Jew me, Sue me / Kick me, Kike me — were so central that they only seemed intended to create hurt and controversy.

But in the 1990s it is rappers who have dominated the music charts with records in which hate and violence are equated with getting respect and being in control of one's life. In the wake of the Los Angeles riots of 1992, the kind of rap that has gotten the most attention from the mainstream media has been that of a performer like Ice-T, whose song "Cop Killer" includes the chorus:

> COP KILLER, it's better you than me.
> COP KILLER, fuck police brutality!
> COP KILLER, I know your family's grievin'
> (FUCK 'EM)
> COP KILLER, but tonight we get even.

Defenders of rap, such as University of Pennsylvania literature professor Houston Baker, point out that mainstream criticism of rap tends to ignore its social roots as well as the "strategies of resistance" it offers young black men. But what has been most significant about rap in the 1990s is the degree to which its violence and anger have been turned inward and in the form of "gangsta rap" glorified a machismo that leaves no tenderness for anyone. The recent slayings of rap stars Tupac Shakur and Notorious B.I.G. have not only enhanced their reputations, they have brought new fans to rap, which in 1996 grew by 33 percent to account for 9 percent of the $12.5 billion music industry.[20]

Drive-by shootings and black on black gang violence are central to rap, and from there the hate spirals every which way. Anyone who is different is seen as hostile and, as Ice Cube's "Black Korea" makes clear, immediately put in the category of an enemy who deserves to be brutalized:

> Oriental one-penny countin' . . .
>
> follow me up and down your market . . .
>
> Pay respect to the black fist or we'll burn your
>
> store right down.

For black women — "hos" and "bitches" in nineties rap — the judgments are even harsher. "I think a lot of misogynous rap is similar to crack," the black feminist writer bell hooks recently observed. "It gives people a false sense of agency. It gives them a sense that they have power over their lives when they don't." Hers is a view that rappers themselves have been undeterred by. At the 1993 meeting of the National Association of Black Journalists, Bushwick Bill of the rap group Geto Boys touched off a bitter explosion when, in response to the question why so much rap music denigrates black women, he said, "I call women bitches and hos because all the women I've met since I've been out here are bitches and hos."[21]

Bushwick Bill's response was a match for the direction gangsta rap has taken in the nineties. Where women are concerned, it doesn't just describe "the way things are." It revels in abuse. "She's gone now so it's time to make the switch. So who will be my next gangsta bitch?" asks the narrator of Apache's "Gangsta Bitch" after his gun-toting girlfriend is hauled off to jail. She is lucky; at least her boyfriend is willing to let her go. More commonly in gangsta rap it is not enough to use a woman and then walk away from her. The great pleasure comes from sexually humiliating her. Typical is 2 Live Crew's "The Fuck Shop":

> Let me fill you with somethin milky and white
> 'Cause I'm gonna slay you rough and painful . . .

Or N.W.A. in "Findum, Fuckum, and Flee":

> When the pussy holes are open, ready to fuck
>   until my dick is raw . . .
> So come here, bitch, and lick up the, lick up the,
>   lick up the dick!

Or Just Ice with this warning:

> Don't try to get too close
> And try to kiss me and hug me
> Start to caress me, then say you love me.
> 'Cause I don't feel shit
> It's only rhythm that I ride
> The only love I got is psychopathic homicide.[22]

■ ■ ■

It is difficult to imagine rap having its current appeal a generation ago, when the civil rights movement was at its peak and fundamental social change seemed at hand. None of the cruelty that is so central to rap would have made sense in the milieu created by sixties politics. Like the new savagery of which it is a part, rap depends on the loss of hope and the loss of a culture in which compassion is a vital ingredient.

Nobody has more thoroughly captured this change — and the brutal aesthetic it has made possible — than the film director Quentin Tarantino in his Academy Award–winning *Pulp Fiction* of 1994. The film's principal characters are two Los Angeles hit men, Vincent Vega (John Travolta) and Jules Winnfield (Samuel L. Jackson), their crime boss, Marsellus Wallace (Ving Rhames), his wife (Uma Thurman), and Butch (Bruce Willis), a boxer who is supposed to throw a fight Marsellus has bet on but who instead double-crosses him and knocks out his opponent. Their stories are told separately and out of sequence, with the result, as film critic Sarah Kerr pointed out in her review of *Pulp Fiction*, that instead of a protagonist the film has a milieu — underground Los Angeles in the 1990s.[23]

The core of *Pulp Fiction* lies in what happens after Vincent and Jules accidentally murder someone who has double-crossed their boss. The murder takes place in a car when Vincent's gun goes off by mistake. In order to avoid getting caught, he and Jules take refuge in the house of Vincent's friend Jimmie, played by Tarantino himself. The scene that follows is not, however, at all suspenseful in the way we would expect. It is driven by Vincent's and

Jules's need to clean themselves and their car before Jimmie's wife returns from work. Jimmie insists his wife will divorce him if she finds a dead body in the house, and it is fear of her arrival that drives events. The episode at first seems filled with irony — a brutal murder juxtaposed with the killers' need to achieve the appearance of normalcy. But the murder itself (we don't see the body) is never a serious concern. Instead we get a hip version of the kind of situation comedy television has traditionally supplied.[24]

The crazed disorder that follows the murder is the sort the *I Love Lucy* show specialized in during the 1950s. A show would begin with Lucy doing something silly, like getting her finger caught in a bowling ball, and the rest of the half-hour would revolve around Lucy trying to hide her predicament from Ricky. In the midst of Lucy's clowning, it never made sense to ask why she was so fearful of Ricky's disapproval, and in the cleaning-up scene in *Pulp Fiction*, we also don't worry about deeper questions. Ruthless as hit men, Vincent and Jules are total flops at cleaning up. They worry that without Lava soap they won't be able to clean the blood off their hands, and they bicker over who will wipe the blood off the car windows and who will get the brain matter out of the back seat. Their final humiliation comes when they must take off all their clothes and be hosed down by Jimmie. Standing there naked, they are like children who have gotten themselves so covered in mud while playing that they cannot be allowed in the house to shower. When they get dressed, it is not in the funereal black suits they wore when they did the killing but in swimming trunks and T-shirts lent by Jimmie.

Their transformation is now complete. They have been turned from badasses into "dorks," as Jimmie puts it. At this point it is impossible to imagine Vincent and Jules as brutal hit men, just as it is finally impossible to feel upset about the murder, rape, and drug dealing that underlie virtually every scene in *Pulp Fiction*. Tarantino's film company, A Band Apart, is named after French director Jean-Luc Godard's 1964 film *Bande à Part* and its story of two hoods and a femme fatale. But unlike Godard, Tarantino has not used his reworking of the pulp aesthetic to struggle with a series of philosophical issues. His comedy isn't designed to bring us up short just as we are enjoying ourselves. The film's savage pleasures supply not only the violence we see but the laughter used as anesthesia to undermine any moral revulsion we might feel about the violence.[25]

It is a strategy that has made Tarantino the most talked-about Hollywood film director of the nineties, but in many ways Tarantino has done nothing in regard to making violence pleasurable that the public has not finally shown it is prepared to do on its own. We need only ask ourselves how over the course of 1995 the O. J. Simpson trial, despite the racial sores it exposed, became the leading news event, sports event, and entertainment event of the year. Certainly it was not the pathos of the trial — the deaths of a young mother and an even younger actor —

that packed the courtroom or by the trial's end were responsible for thirty O.J.-related books, "I Killed Nicole" T-shirts, "The Dancing Itos," and the Internet list of O. J. Simpson jokes with seventeen orange juice puns and thirteen gags featuring Hertz. What made a seat at the O. J. Simpson trial the hottest ticket in Los Angeles and allowed CNN to charge up to $24,000 per thirty-second commercial during its telecasts was the sight of a celebrity accused of murder suddenly made vulnerable, his private sexual life exposed, the details of his alleged crime documented with color photos. In the atmosphere created by the new savagery, it was easy for most viewers to be enthralled rather than repulsed by such a combination of events.[26]

Much harder to know is where it all ends. In explaining the violence that drives the rioters at the end of *The Day of the Locust*, Nathanael West cited the "lynchings, murders, sex crimes" that they were exposed to every day in newspapers and movies. "This daily diet made sophisticates of them. The sun is a joke. Oranges can't titillate their jaded palates. Nothing can ever be violent enough," he sardonically observed. So it is with us and the savage pleasures. Like the stories of fires and gang shootings that are the staples of the eleven o'clock news in every large city, they are our cultural ballast. We no longer know how to do without them.[27]

PART TWO
Divided We Stand

3 Corporate Darwinism

ON THE FIRST BUSI-
ness day of 1996, AT&T announced the biggest single job
cut in the history of the telephone industry. Over the next
three years, the company declared, it would eliminate
40,000 jobs and take a $6 billion charge against earnings
in order to split itself into three different companies.
Downsizing on such a scale would have been front-page
news at any time. But in 1996 what brought AT&T the
coverage it got — "Corporate Killers," the headline on
Newsweek's cover story read — was that its decision to
downsize removed any lingering doubts about corporate
culture in the 1990s. The firings said that from a business
perspective it was perfectly all right for a thriving company
to shed thousands of workers, watch its stock prices shoot
up as a consequence, and then reward its CEO and top executives with stock options that were even more valuable
than before.[1]

In contrast to General Motors, which in 1991 set the

record for the single biggest downsizing of the decade when it announced plans to cut its workforce by more than 70,000, AT&T downsized when the company was healthy and most of its business was profitable. The day after the announcement, its stock prices went up more than two points, to $67.38, and for its CEO, Robert Allen, the result was a pay package that by the end of February was estimated to have risen from $6.7 million to $16 million.[2]

Making AT&T's downsizing seem even more ruthless was its own history. Until 1984, when an antitrust suit originally brought by the government in 1981 forced AT&T to break itself up into a series of smaller regional companies, the company known as Ma Bell was very protective of its workers. Lifetime employment and good benefits were the norm. Many employees rose through the ranks, and layoffs were rare. As the first page of AT&T's 1947 employees' manual explained, "The company endeavors to take care of its employees throughout their working careers, and beyond. In return, it naturally expects employees to be genuinely concerned with the welfare of the business and to feel personally responsible for its reputation and continuing success."[3]

It is not, however, necessary to sentimentalize the past at AT&T or suggest that it was free of conflict in order to understand the ruthlessness of its 1996 downsizing. The updated corporate Darwinism AT&T used to explain its firings made its thinking clear from the start. A century earlier John D. Rockefeller did not hesitate to observe of the business ethics of Standard Oil, "The growth of a large business is merely a survival of the fittest, the working out of a law of nature and a law of God," and in an open letter sent to all AT&T employees on February 26, 1996, AT&T CEO Robert Allen used a similar defense — he was assuring the competitive survival of AT&T — to justify the lucrative stock options he was receiving while his workforce was being slashed. "We all know the times demand a radical transformation of our business," Allen wrote. The choice was clear: "Make the necessary, even painful, changes today or forfeit the future. Some of America's most sturdy and successful corporations were unceremoniously humbled when they failed to recognize — or react to — inexorable change that threatened their markets."[4]

Allen left it to others to explain how the necessary and painful changes he described would affect middle managers and nonsupervisory workers. But as AT&T's downsizing began in early January, it quickly became clear that the company's determination to operate from a "position of strength" would leave everyone except key executives vulnerable. The process of cutting 13 percent of a workforce of 303,000 was carried out literally by the book, the one-hundred-page *AT&T Force Management Program Manual* that outlined the exact procedures supervisors were expected to take in laying off workers. First, each worker was asked to fill out a résumé outlining his experience and skills. Then his supervisor was asked to file an Employee Assessment Summary, rating the employee's job skills, leadership, and teamwork capacity on a scale of one to four. After that, the résumé and assessment summary were placed before a roundtable meeting of the senior executives of the employee's department, who decided whether the employee would be kept or let go. Under the rules, at least one of the managers at the roundtable had to know the employee personally, and to make sure the discussion was as fair as possible, it was moderated by a facilitator or neutral observer. But that was it. The roundtable decisions were final, unless AT&T's lawyers found in them a pattern that might subject AT&T to lawsuits for racial or sexual discrimination.[5]

"The idea is that everybody has been asked to step out into a parking lot," Adele Ambrose, a spokeswoman for AT&T told the *New York Times*. It was an analogy that in the picture it drew of thousands of AT&T employees standing around a parking lot in the middle of winter, while inside the warm buildings where they worked their supervisors made decisions on whether they would be allowed back in, suggested cold indifference on AT&T's part. It was not a false impression. "The days of corporate loyalty are gone. We are all becoming freelance workers," Brenda Barbour, the director of AT&T's Washington Area Career Resource Center, concluded was the best advice she could give to the fired workers who were her clients. At AT&T headquarters, vice president James Meadows was even blunter in spelling out the assumptions behind AT&T's mass downsizing. The old social contract that said if you come with us you have lifetime employment, Meadows declared, was "in the wastebasket." In the 1990s AT&T's relationship with its employees was just the opposite. "People need to look at themselves as self-employed, as vendors who come to this company to sell their skills," Meadows explained. In the new social contract neither loyalty nor years of service was paramount. The only consideration that mattered was a worker's ongoing relevance to AT&T. He or she was not hired to have a permanent job but to complete projects and after that be hired or fired depending on the projects and fields of work that materialized. Nothing, in short, could be counted on over the long haul. In a changing economy a company like AT&T could not be expected to make long-term commitments to its workforce and still meet its own needs.[6]

■　■　■

In a *New York Times* op ed, "How to Avoid These Lay-offs?" published just two days after AT&T's announcement, a worried secretary of labor Robert Reich wrote, "AT&T's stunning announcement on the first business day of 1996 that it would permanently lay off 40,000 employees raises profound questions about the private sector's ability to take on more responsibility for Americans' economic well-being." Reich's remarks were not surprising. As a political economist at Harvard's John F. Kennedy School of Government, Reich had for many years been writing about the problems of retraining workers and of the difficulties for the economy of companies that no longer saw their interests as bound up with the prosperity of the country.[7]

In the 1990s it has not, however, been only liberal economists like Reich, with roots primarily in the academic community, who have worried about where corporate Darwinism — with its mass layoffs and assaults on workers' wages — is taking the country. Within the Federal Reserve and on Wall Street fears have also run high. In the summer of 1995, Federal Reserve Board Chairman Alan Greenspan warned Congress that the increasing inequality of incomes posed a "major threat to our society," and over the last three years that theme has been sounded again and again. At the start of a 1995 colloquium on wage trends in America, William J. McDonough, the president of the Federal Reserve Bank of New York, observed that as a result of the growing disparity between income groups in the United States, "We are forced to face the question whether we will be able to go forward together as a unified society with a confident outlook or as a society of diverse economic groups suspicious of both the future and each other."[8]

Two months later, in a speech entitled "Requiem for a Democrat," delivered at Wake Forest University's Babcock School of Management, Felix Rohatyn, a senior partner at Lazard Frères and the former chairman of New York's Municipal Assistance Corporation, was even more emphatic about the dangers of the changes business was imposing. "What is occurring is a huge transfer of wealth from lower-skilled middle-class American workers to the owners of capital assets and to a new technological aristocracy with a large element of compensation tied to stock values," Rohatyn declared. "As a result, the institutional relationship created by the mutual loyalty of employers and employees in most American businesses has been badly frayed."[9]

A year after Rohatyn's speech, in a report he called "Worker Backlash: The Dark Side of America's Productivity-Led Recovery," Stephen Roach, the chief economist for Morgan Stanley, was gloomier still in his assessment of what was happening as a consequence of the "unprecedented squeeze in labor costs" that companies were carrying out during a time of rising profits and productivity. "For the modern-day American worker, the angst of the 1990s is without precedent," Roach warned investors, and it was likely to produce a backlash. Voters would look to political remedies to change the business practices that were making their lives worse no matter how hard they worked.[10]

The backlash Roach and others on Wall Street warned business about has not, however, materialized in the workplace or in new regulations. On the contrary, workers have taken a look at what is going on in the economy and decided that it makes sense to hunker down and hope to get by. As Harvard historian David Herbert Donald observed in early 1996, "You read that 40,000 people are laid off at AT&T and a shiver goes down your back that says, 'That could be me.'" Such fears are not exaggerated, and with the Clinton administration engaged in a massive government downsizing of its own — "Today, the federal workforce is 200,000 employees smaller than the day I took office," the president proudly announced in his 1996 State of the Union Address — it is hard for workers to imagine help is coming. An estimated 43 million jobs have been lost in the United States since 1979, and as the *New York Times* discovered in its seven-part series "The Downsizing of America," most people have had a personal encounter with job loss. Since 1980 in one-third of all households a family member has lost a job, while 40 percent more know a relative, friend, or neighbor who was laid off. Indeed, as a University of Michigan Study of Income Dynamics covering this same period found, the economy's volatility has meant that all sources of job change have been more frequent over the last fifteen years — with not only higher layoffs but outright firings double what they were.[11]

Among blue-collar workers, who have been steadily losing out in jobs and wages since the 1970s, the fear of challenging an employer is reflected in an unwillingness to strike. In 1995 there were just thirty-two strikes, the lowest figure since World War II. With union membership at just 14 percent overall — 11 percent in private industry — workers see themselves as enormously vulnerable, especially to companies anxious to globalize their production. As Jay Mazur, the president of the Union of Needletrades, Industrial, and Textile Employees, acknowledged, "Workers are very concerned about people taking their jobs away if they strike."[12]

Among white-collar workers, who by 1993 had more

unemployment than blue-collar workers, the fears are just as great. Few of the old safeguards work as they once did. Unlike the 1980s, in the 1990s workers with at least some college education make up the majority of people whose jobs were eliminated, and higher-paid workers, those earning $50,000 or more, now account for twice the share of lost jobs that they did in the 1980s. For these white-collar workers, asking for a raise or confronting an over-demanding boss is out of the question. The constant workplace fears that Scott Adams describes in his syndi-cated cartoon *Dilbert*, which recounts the office life of a computer operator whose daily struggles come down to a desperate battle for survival, are theirs — but without the compensating jokes. For them there is even a new genre of business book — typified by G. J. Meyer's *Executive Blues* — in which the central character is not a business success but someone who learns to survive a midcareer firing.[13]

"You don't feel as if you have any control. You feel completely helpless," a longtime AT&T worker, who asked that her name be withheld, told me after she got through the company's January downsizing. "I feel I have survived by luck. Just by luck and being in the right place at the right time," she said. Her anxiety is mirrored by a 1996 *New York Times* poll that showed what people work-ing or wanting to work would do for a job: 93 percent said they would get more training or education; 82 percent said they would work longer hours; 71 percent said they would take fewer vacation days; 53 percent said they would accept smaller benefits; 49 percent said they would challenge the boss less often; and 44 percent said they would take a lower salary.[14]

.   .   .

Especially for large corporations, such job anxiety has made the cost of doing business cheaper. But equally significant, over the course of the 1990s, it has been paralleled by the rise of a business philosophy that, as in the Gilded Age, has sought to justify an economy in which the gap between those at the top and everyone else grows wider and wider. A century ago the spokesmen for that Gilded Age business culture and the social Darwinism that was its intellectual backbone were widely known. They included a minister like William Lawrence, the Episcopal bishop of Massachusetts, who assured his congregation that "the race is to the strong" and "Godliness is in league with riches," as well as an academic like Yale sociologist William Graham Sumner, who believed that we owed our progress to the "captains of industry" and the social organization they made possible. Within industry the voices of social Darwinism were equally prominent. They included John D. Rockefeller and steel magnate Andrew Carnegie, who in his famous essay "The Gospel of Wealth" argued that the "best interests of the race" were promoted by a system that "inevitably gives wealth to the few."[15]

A century later the defenders of corporate Darwinism don't come so well known or with such impressive credentials, but the corporate culture they have managed to establish is as coherent and ruthless as that of the 1890s, and it has helped create in America the widest gap between rich and poor of any industrialized nation. The top 1 percent of the nation's households now controls almost one-third (30.4 percent) of the nation's net worth. The next 9 percent hold another third (36.8 percent) while the remaining 90 percent struggle to live on 32.8 percent of the wealth. How different the new corporate culture is from the corporate culture America embraced in its recent past may be seen when we look back at the 1950s, when two mutually related views of corporate culture reigned. The first, epitomized by Frank Abrams, the chairman of Standard Oil of New Jersey, held, "'The job of management is to maintain an equitable and working balance among . . . stockholders, employees, customers and the public at large." A decision that undermined this balance would ultimately jeopardize a company's long-term success, Abrams insisted. The second view, put forward by "Engine Charlie" Wilson, the president of General Motors, during his 1953 confirmation hearings to become secretary of defense, was that the interests of the United States and the interests of its largest corporations were tied together. When asked whether he would be capable of making a decision that helped the country but hurt GM, Wilson replied that such a conflict would never occur. "I cannot conceive of one because for years I thought what was good for our country was good for General Motors, and vice versa. The difference did not exist. Our company is too big. It goes with the welfare of the country."[16]

In the 1990s the bedrock of corporate philosophy has been the belief that a company has no higher allegiance than to itself and its shareholders. Neither country nor public nor employees count as much as shareholders do. As Al Dunlap, currently CEO of the Sunbeam Corporation and a man who has been involved in the restructuring of nine different companies, put it in a recent *Harper's* magazine symposium, "The responsibility of the CEO is to deliver shareholder value. Period. It's the shareholders who own the corporation. They take all the risk." For Dunlap, getting tied up with larger social issues, let alone worrying about the impact a company's policies are having on the country, is a waste of time. "The job of industry is to become competitive — not to be a social experiment. God help us if we pass legislation to make American companies less productive and compromise our global competitiveness," he insists, and in his autobiography, *Mean Business*, he leaves no room for doubt about his willingness to be mean. For Dunlap, concern for the company's stakeholders — its employees and the surrounding community — is sentimental nonsense. So is corporate philanthropy, most human resources work, and striving for racial diversity on the board of directors. And so is worrying about firing workers. "A company is not your high school or college alma mater," he reminds his readers. "You can outsource just about anything today."[17]

How deeply Dunlap's thinking has become business orthodoxy in the nineties was reflected in a 1996 *Wall Street Journal* op ed, "Corporate America, Mind Your

Own Business," written by Herb Stein, the former chairman of the President's Council on Economic Advisers and a fellow of the American Enterprise Institute. In language that picked up where Dunlap had left off in the *Harper's* symposium, Stein complained, "Corporate executives are held to be narrow-minded if they pay attention only to maximizing profits for the benefit of shareholders and ignore the other stakeholders." It was crucial, Stein insisted, for CEOs to ignore such accusations and not be diverted from their focus on profit. "Corporations," he concluded, "should not accept responsibility for doing anything the government asks them to do. More specifically, they should not accept responsibility for doing something they would not want the government to do in the hope of thereby preventing the government from doing it."[18]

What such a belief in the primacy of the shareholders means for the culture of an individual company was reflected at IBM after Louis Gerstner became its CEO in 1993. Under Thomas Watson, Jr., the son of IBM's founder, the company had held doggedly to its three core beliefs: pursue excellence, provide the best customer service, and above all show employees "respect for the individual." Under Gerstner the three core beliefs were changed to eight corporate principles. On the new list, number one was "The marketplace is the driving force behind everything we do." At the bottom, as number eight, was "We are sensitive to the needs of all employees and to the communities in which we operate."[19]

In the 1990s the ultimate significance of a corporate

culture that makes allegiance to the shareholder so dominant is that anything goes. Downsizing, whether it means that individual lives are shattered or worker morale is undermined, is justified as long as expenses are lowered. At the heart of the new corporate Darwinism has been the belief by CEOs that there is no reason for them to feel responsible for either the decline of the middle class (from 57 to 47 percent of the country since 1970) or the rise of the working poor (from 39 to 45 percent during this same period). At AT&T the joke making the rounds after its 1996 layoffs were announced was that the company's initials would soon stand for Allen and Two Temps. But in terms of the 1990s, AT&T's downsizing represents a general pattern. Between 1991 and 1995 IBM cut 85,000 employees, General Motors 74,000, Sears 50,000, Boeing 30,000, NYNEX 22,000, GTE 17,000, Union Carbide 14,000, Bank of America 12,000, and Pacific Telesis 12,000.[20]

As telling as the downsizing, moreover, have been the cost-cutting strategies that have accompanied it. During the summer of 1996, when a public furor developed over the discovery that sweatshop labor was used in producing entertainer Kathie Lee Gifford's line of clothes, there was much discussion over businesses making huge profits from brutalizing exploitation. But what has come to be taken as a norm is the practice of companies doing whatever they can to avoid paying ongoing American wages. Think of it "as if you were starting a plant on the moon," Michael Rothbaum, the CEO of Harwood Industries observed after moving his clothing manufacturing from Virginia to Central America, where weekly take-home pay averages around $25 and medical benefits are not a requirement.[21]

In blue-collar and white-collar work, outsourcing has become a standard way of avoiding having a well-paid workforce that does all of a company's work. At General Motors a seventeen-day strike arose in 1996 over the company's decision to buy brake parts from nonunion suppliers, but General Motors, which as part of its strike settlement paid the affected brake workers $1,700 each in compensation, never backed off from its commitment to outsourcing, and neither have a growing number of businesses. Some companies, such as Nike and Mattel, don't operate their own factories. Others have found that even with high-tech computer operations it is cheaper to hire English-speaking programmers in foreign countries at much lower wages. As Thomas Watrous, the managing partner of Andersen Consulting's office in Manila, observed, "There's really a strong parallel to the 1960s and 1970s, when U.S. manufacturers sent everything offshore. The difference is that it is being done electronically."[22]

For companies that in the 1990s want the benefits of outsourcing without going abroad, it is also possible to get the same results in house. Increasingly, temporary employees, who don't get a health plan, retirement pay, or vacations are being used by companies to avoid hiring full-time workers. Often these temps are the very employees the companies downsized, now hired back as contract workers to do their old jobs on far less favorable terms. By

1993 temps filled 16 percent of all new jobs. In addition many companies have found that it is cheaper to take advantage of the H-1B visa program, which allows 65,000 "specialty occupation" workers to enter the country each year for stays of up to six years. The workers are supposed to be paid the prevailing wages and not used as strikebreakers, but the Labor Department does not have the personnel to check on how H-1Bs are used, and in the 1990s they have become a plentiful supply of inexpensive labor — "technobraceros," the high-tech equivalent of migrant farm workers and a hedge against white-collar discontent. Employment agencies called body shops, which specialize in supplying skilled foreign workers for American companies, have even made it unnecessary for businesses to go overseas to recruit. All a business has to do is want a bargain-basement workforce.[23]

And they do. Inseparable from the save-at-any-cost emphasis of corporate culture in the nineties is the corollary belief that workers are a contingent rather than an organic part of business. At AT&T vice president James Meadows reflected this view when he observed that in the new AT&T workers needed to think of themselves as self-employed, and over the course of the 1990s this idea has come to be expressed in even harsher terms. In his book *Corporate Executions*, management consultant Alan Downs, writing from the perspective of an employer in the nineties, noted that workers are best seen as a consumable commodity. "You buy the people power you need to keep the business running. When you discover that you have more people than you need, you stop buying as many," Downs observed. "Employees are interchangeable components that can be plugged in wherever and whenever they are needed. They are disposable as well. When the immediate demand for their services has subsided, they can be discarded."[24]

For liberal economists, taking such an approach to workers is dehumanizing. In his 1994 study *Lean and Mean*, economics professor Bennett Harrison described such a strategy as the "low road" to profits, a path by which managers try to beat out the competition by cheapening labor costs and scrimping on training. Two years later the late David Gordon, in his parallel study, *Fat and Mean*, extended Harrison's low-road metaphor with a description of what he called the "stick" strategy of business management, in which wages are lowered and workers are made to fear for their jobs.[25]

What is so revealing about business culture in the 1990s is that its most ardent practicioners feel no need to deny they are doing exactly what critics like Harrison and Gordon say they are doing. Indeed, they take pride in it. Currently one of the most lucrative business seminars in the country is that of the Center for Creative Leadership. At the heart of the materials participants in the weeklong seminar receive is an article entitled "Leadership in an Age of Layoffs." Written by David Noer, the center's senior vice president, the article emphasizes that we have left behind an employer-employee era in which companies believed "good performance should be rewarded with

promotion and management should take care of employees."
In the new era, such assumptions are dated, and it is necessary for businesses to act accordingly, Noer argues. To get
ahead and develop "a truly flexible workforce," it is essential for organizations to "remove artificial pay, benefits and
status distinctions among employee classifications." In the
business world of the nineties, Noer contends, "All employees are now, in a sense, temporary," and they should
be treated as such. His final advice, in case workers don't
get the point, is that companies should drive their vulner-
ability home to them. "Don't," he urges, "provide rec-
reational opportunities if the community already does.
Don't offer group purchasing plans. Don't sponsor clubs
or social events like picnics. All of these promote dependency in one form or another."[26]

Noer's advice doesn't come cheap. The Center for
Creative Leadership charges managers and executives
$2,900 for its weeklong seminars. But there has been no
reluctance by CEOs and key managers to take advice like
Noer's. The final article of faith in the corporate culture of
the nineties is that the lion's share of the spoils should go
to those at the top, that in a period of widespread downsizing and cost-cutting there is no need for CEOs and
those in the upper levels of management to share in the
sacrifices and take proportional reductions in their pay.
In 1992, the last year for which complete corporate sta-
tistics are available from the IRS, America's corporations paid their top executives $221 billion — a total that,
as Donald Barlett and James Steele point out in their

1996 *Philadelphia Inquirer* series, "America: Who Stole the Dream?" exceeds the combined incomes of every working person and family earning less than $50,000 a year in Arkansas, Kansas, Missouri, Oregon, Pennsylvania, and Wisconsin. What's more, for most of these executives special deferred compensation plans and protected retirement packages guaranteed that, in contrast to everyone else in the companies they worked for, they wouldn't have to worry about bankruptcy or anything else going wrong. They would always be protected.[27]

When Robert Allen was confronted by Lesley Stahl of *60 Minutes* on the fairness of his huge pay package at a time when so many workers at AT&T were being fired in order to cut costs, he was furious. "I will not debate with anybody the difference between what a front-line worker gets and what a CEO of a company gets," Allen told Stahl. "I don't think it's hurting the country. I don't see how it's hurting the country." Allen's view is reflected throughout the corporate culture of the nineties. When Chemical Bank and Chase Manhattan merged in 1995, they were able to reduce expenses by cutting 12,000 jobs from their combined banks, but in the process of cutting, it never occurred to them to reduce the number of outside directors. Similarly, Dial Corporation has dramatically cut its employee payroll in recent years, but it has felt free to use these savings to invest lavishly in executive salaries, corporate jets, and a new headquarters.[28]

The final proof of the corporate culture's new ruthlessness lies, however, in CEO salaries in the nineties. In

1974 the typical CEO made thirty-five times the average worker's pay. By the nineties the figure was one hundred and fifty times and climbing, compared to a sixteen-to-one ratio in Japan and a twenty-one to one ratio in Germany. And in big companies often the ratio did not tell the full story. In 1995, in seventy-six of the nation's one hundred and fifty largest companies, the median CEO salary and cash bonus rose 15 percent to over $2 million, and at the highest ranks, the salaries were off the charts: $203 million for Michael Eisner of Walt Disney, $49 million for Sanford Weill of the Travelers, $23 million for Roberto Goizueta of Coca-Cola, and $22 million for Jack Welch of General Electric.[29]

In a country in which most people still believe that the ideal economy is one in which, as President John Kennedy argued, a rising tide lifts all boats, it requires a special toughness for CEOs to argue that they deserve what they are getting these days, but in the 1990s that has not been a problem. Very much part of corporate culture over the last seven years has been the cultivation by CEOs of the hard-boiled image. At Cypress Semiconductors T. J. Rodgers, its CEO, went out of his way to tell a nun who had publicly challenged him to put more women and minorities on his board that she should get down from her "moral high horse." At IBM Louis Gerstner has made a point of telling his managers they should not feel "entitled" to their jobs. Other CEOs, like the stars of professional wrestling, have cultivated nicknames designed to emphasize their meanness. Al Dunlap became known as "Chainsaw Al" for his willingness to make brutal job cuts, and at General Electric Jack Welch acquired the nickname "Neutron Jack" because he fires workers while leaving the buildings they once occupied standing.[30]

•   ■   ■

A comparison with the 1950s, when a CEO like "Engine Charlie" Wilson of General Motors was nicknamed for the products he turned out is again revealing. What the comparison points to, beyond differences in style and modesty, is the degree to which being a cutting-edge executive in the 1990s has little to do with product and everything to do with suppression of wages. In his 1996 memoir *Time Present, Time Past*, retiring Senator Bill Bradley spoke directly to this issue in a passage discussing the problems that his constituents were having making a living. "Why this harsh treatment of the middle class? The answer is simple — because they are weak and the boss is strong," Bradley wrote.[31]

In the end, however, the most convincing proof of what the corporate Darwinism of the 1990s has meant is reflected in the behavior of the stock market. In 1996, in the face of seemingly good news — government reports of a drop in the unemployment rate — the market twice reacted as if catastrophe were at hand, plunging 171 points in March and 115 points in July. Investors understood, as the corporate culture had been saying all along, that what was good for Main Street was bad for Wall Street and profit taking. It was a strategic ruthlessness that cut jobs and salaries that paid the big dividends.[32]

As for Main Street, it has had the lessons of down-sizing driven home in a very concrete way, as suburbs and company towns that depended on corporations have found themselves stuck with abandoned office buildings and falling real estate prices. In Morristown, New Jersey, where AT&T once dominated civic culture, it now domi-nates civic anxiety. The newest kaffeeklatsch is a support group organized by the spouses of the unemployed, and at the Presbyterian Church of Morristown, a fund originally designed for women abandoned by their husbands is now being tapped to help unemployed middle managers keep up their mortgage payments. For the town's mayor, a re-tired stockbroker, it has all been a shock. "There is such a thing as capitalism with a heart, and then there's Marie Antoinette capitalism," he recently observed. "Most big corporations today aren't interested in capitalism with a heart."[33]

4 Racial Payback

WHEN NEW YORK talk-show host Bob Grant heard that the plane carrying Commerce Secretary Ron Brown and a group of American businessmen had crashed and that only one person might have survived, he did not let the news cramp the style of his on-air monologue. Race was a staple for Grant, and blacks a prime target. Depending on his mood, he called them anything from "screaming savages" to "subhumanoids." I have a "hunch that Brown is the one survivor," Grant told his listeners with mock sadness. "Maybe," he went on, "it's because at heart I'm a pessimist."[1]

Grant's joke about Brown, the most prominent African American in President Clinton's cabinet, did get him fired from his job at WABC-AM by the station's new owners, the Disney Company. But two weeks later Grant was back on the air at rival station WOR-AM, and the station manager, Robert Bruno, was crowing about his good fortune in acquiring a talk-show star with Grant's ratings. "He may not be a choirboy, but he's going to get the job done," Bruno bragged to the press.[2]

For Grant fans, there was nothing new about the Brown controversy. It was vintage Bob Grant. But in terms of the racial climate of the 1990s, Grant's ongoing popularity and immediate reward with a new job are telling. They point up the degree to which in the 1990s racial meanness has come to take on a life of its own. From black church burnings, reminiscent of those that haunted the country during the Mississippi Freedom Summer of 1964, to bumper stickers that complain "Don't Blame Us, We Voted for Jefferson Davis," the divide between whites and blacks has not only widened over the decade. It has widened in ways that increasingly make racial payback our response of first resort.[3]

※　■　■

The shift in the thinking of white voters that would give the racial meanness of the nineties a firm base became apparent to pollsters during the campaign to pass the Civil Rights Act of 1991. In an effort to secure support for the bill, the liberal Leadership Conference on Civil Rights commissioned a poll to find out voters' racial attitudes. The Leadership Conference was shocked by the results. White voters no longer saw civil rights organizations and their proponents as "addressing generalized discrimination." Instead, such groups were seen as pressing the "narrow" concerns of "particularized" groups. As Celinda Lake, one of the authors of the study, conceded, the advocates of civil rights had "lost the advantage" they once had had with the public.[4]

A month later in a *New York Times* interview, Harvard Afro-American studies professor Cornel West addressed the seriousness of the problem. "The power of the civil rights movement under Martin Luther King was its universalism," West observed. "Now, instead of the civil rights movement being viewed as a moral crusade for freedom, it's become an expression of a particular interest group. Once you lose that moral high ground, all you have is a power struggle, and that has never been a persuasive means for the weaker to deal with the stronger."[5]

By mid-decade, poll after poll reinforced West's assessment of what the change in white attitudes meant for blacks. A 1993 survey by the National Science Foundation found white liberals and conservatives growing closer and closer in their negative assessment of blacks. As the authors of the report reluctantly acknowledged, "The most striking result is the sheer frequency with which negative characterizations of blacks are quite openly expressed throughout the white general population." Fifty-one percent of conservatives and 45 percent of liberals agreed that blacks were aggressive or violent; 44 percent of conservatives and 41 percent of liberals said they were boastful. Overall, 34 percent of conservatives and 28 percent of liberals had a high level of belief in the negative stereotypes of blacks.[6]

Two years later, in 1995, a survey sponsored by the *Washington Post*, the Kaiser Family Foundation, and Harvard University showed that white attitudes toward blacks had hardened even more. Fifty-eight percent of whites now saw the breakdown of the black family as the major cause of problems in the black community, while only 38 percent cited racism as a major obstacle. For these whites, there was, it followed, little that could or should be done to provide blacks with additional help; two-thirds said the federal government had no responsibility to make certain that blacks have jobs and incomes equal to whites.[7]

What surveys showed whites were thinking, the culture showed whites were also doing. In 1996 the petroleum giant Texaco, the nation's fourteenth largest company, agreed to spend more than $176 million to settle the most costly racial bias suit in history. What prompted Texaco to settle the case, which it had fought for two years, was public disclosure of a taped conversation in which its top executives didn't just speak disparagingly of Texaco's African-American employees, but in the case of its treasurer, Robert Ulrich, described them as "black jelly beans" and in the case of its personnel director, Richard Lundwell, explained their low status within the company by joking, "All the black jelly beans seemed to be glued to the bottom of the bag." Suddenly it was no longer possible for Texaco to deny that its promotion policies (just six — 0.7 percent — of its highest-paid employees are black) were prejudiced or that it had a corporate culture in which racism prevailed.[8]

Over the course of the 1990s it has not, however, taken anything as complicated as the Texaco discrimination suit to reveal how extensive our current racial meanness has become. Its perpetrators have gone out of their way to make their feelings known. In Chicago, white school teachers, frustrated with working in a predominantly minority school, amused themselves — and on one occasion gave to their students — an "inner city math exam" that for months had circulated among the nation's public schools as an underground teacher publication. The exam, with questions about cocaine selling, drive-by shootings, and prison, was designed to be a parody of black life. "Rufus is pimping three girls," a typical question read. "If the price is $65 for each trick, how many tricks will each girl have to turn so Rufus can pay for his $800-per-day crack habit?" In New York the Yankees, anxious to move out of their predominantly black and Hispanic Bronx neighborhood, which the team's ownership believes frightens away suburban fans, signaled their thinking about the neighborhood with an interview Richard Kraft, their vice president for community relations, gave to *New York* magazine. In the interview Kraft spoke of those who live around Yankee Stadium as "scavengers" and described the children of the South Bronx as "monkeys," who should not be given free tickets to ball games because they have no sense of "what it's like in a society where things are ordered."[9]

Among young whites, the racial meanness of the nineties has been even rawer, showing up most often as style. In the North the style has meant sudden popularity for Notre Dame baseball caps, because they come with the initials ND, street code for "Niggers Die," and in the South it has meant anti–Malcolm X T-shirts, featuring the Confederate flag accompanied by the slogan "You Wear

Your X, I'll Wear Mine." Even the suburbs have not been spared. At wealthy Greenwich High School in Connecticut, five seniors created a scandal when they slipped into their yearbook a coded message that when spelled out in full read, "All Niggers Die."[10]

It is not the crudest manifestations that have made the racial meanness of the 1990s so formidable, however, but its respectability, its presence in an intellectual and social culture we take seriously. In this regard the 1994 publication of Charles Murray's and the late Richard Herrnstein's *The Bell Curve*, with its focus on low black IQ as the basic reason for black poverty, was a watershed event. The book gave respectability, in the form of a barely disguised biological determinism, to a notion that for decades had been taboo for anyone to say: blacks are an inferior race. Murray and Herrnstein's argument allowed middle-class voters and anyone else with an axe to grind to talk and think like a racist without feeling guilty. One did not have to read *The Bell Curve*'s 872 pages of text and graphs to understand its main premise; it was all laid out in reviews and in excerpted sections of the book.[11]

The Bell Curve has not stood alone in the intellectual race wars of the 1990s. A new lack of restraint has taken over. From Jared Taylor's 1992 study, *Paved with Good Intentions*, with its focus on "the squalor and barbarism of America's cities," to Dinesh D'Souza's 1995 *The End of Racism*, with its description of an urban black America dominated by "behavior that would be regarded as pathological anywhere else," a series of highly influential scholarly books has created an intellectual climate in which one doesn't have to fear being called an Archie Bunker for stating that nothing can be done with large segments of the black community except to isolate them and write them off. When, following the midterm congressional elections of 1994, conservative Gerald Solomon became chairman of the House Rules Committee, his first symbolic gesture was to put up a portrait of the committee's ultra-segregationist past chairman, Howard W. Smith of Virginia. After protests by a group of black representatives, Solomon removed the portrait, but his action was consistent with the racial climate of the 1990s. The kind of racial meanness Smith embodied in the late 1950s and early 1960s has come to set the tone for the present decade.[12]

It is a meanness that rests on the notion that blacks are responsible for their poverty and that neither discrimination nor the disappearance of entry-level jobs is the primary source of their problems. As Jared Taylor put it in *Paved with Good Intentions*, "The disagreeable truth is that many underclass blacks simply refuse to work at low-paying jobs. There is enough welfare money and untaxed incomes in their communities to sustain them." The charge itself is hardly fresh; it was a staple of the Reagan administration's policy throughout the 1980s. But in the 1990s what has made the idea that blacks deserve little sympathy for the job problems they face so powerful is the degree to which it has been combined with praise of new immigrants who *are* making it. From the neoliberal *New Republic* to the conservative *Commentary*, the typical story about blacks and immigrants has become, as former Reagan civil rights commissioner Linda Chavez wrote, one in which "the despair of the former seems all the more intense by contrast to the striving of the latter — as if one group had given up on America even as the other was proving the existence of continued opportunity."[13]

To make matters worse, the picture of blacks striving to avoid work has been accompanied by that of blacks striving to get on welfare. The charge is a familiar one, but in the 1990s it too has been given new power. With only slight modification, the idea that blacks want to be on welfare has become accepted by liberals and reformers, as well as by the right. The groundwork for the change was set by President Clinton in his 1992 campaign, when he declared, "It's time to honor and reward people who play by the rules. This means ending welfare as we know it." The president's aim was to transform welfare to workfare, but what voters heard, and what quickly became central to liberal and neoliberal thinking, was the distinction the president's language drew between those who play by the rules and those who are on welfare. By the mid-1990s it had become standard for an increasingly wide range of policymakers to argue, as welfare reformer Mickey Kaus did, "Welfare is implicated in America's most difficult social problem — the existence of whole neighborhoods, mostly African American, where there are precious few intact working families. Welfare may or may not have caused this underclass, but welfare is clearly what sustains it."[14]

Such attitudes cleared the way for congressional Democrats to vote for, and for the president to sign, the welfare reform act of 1996 (the Personal Responsibility and Work Opportunity Act), ending the federal safeguards for families with dependent children that had been in place since 1935. Even for many on the left, going along with such legislation was no longer a betrayal of the poor. It was simply doing what was needed to force blacks to look for work. A Connecticut law mandating electronic fingerprinting of all welfare recipients summed up the thinking behind Congress's and the president's actions. In contrast to those receiving Social Security or Medicare, those on welfare, the Connecticut law declared by the safeguards it required, could only be viewed as permanent suspects, different from the rest of society.[15]

The final consequence of such thinking is that in the 1990s black crime has come to be seen not as an aberration but as a logical extension of the values on which black culture rests. In a highly publicized 1993 speech, Jesse Jackson confessed, "There is nothing more painful to me at this stage in my life than to walk down the street and hear footsteps and start thinking about robbery — then look around and see somebody white and feel relieved." Millions of whites have also had that reaction. Only instead of feeling Jackson's pain, they have responded with anger, offering no solution to black crime except longer prison sentences and harsher treatment of criminals. "It has now become acceptable to talk about black crime," former New York mayor Ed Koch observed in a *National Review* essay in which he went on to say that when he heard liberals talk about the root causes of crime, he wanted to go to the nearest window, as Peter Finch did in *Network*, and yell, "I'm mad as hell, and I'm not going to take it anymore." In a speech delivered on the Senate floor following the 1992 Los Angeles riots, Bill Bradley, himself a critic of police brutality and a defender of civil rights, addressed this problem directly. Taking, for the moment, the perspective of an angry white voter, he imagined him saying to the young blacks he saw on the street and on nightly television, "You litter the street and deface the subway, and no one, white or black, says stop.... You snatch a purse, you crash a concert, break a telephone booth, and no one, white or black, says stop. You rob a store, rape a jogger, shoot a tourist, and when they catch you — if they catch you — you cry racism."[16]

The feelings Bradley talked about in the summer of 1992 have not only become more frequently discussed since then, they have also become part of public policy. Bill Clinton's decision during the 1992 presidential campaign to fly back to Little Rock for the execution of Ricky Ray Rector, a black Arkansas man convicted of killing a white police officer, was not just symbolic of his determination not to be Willie Hortoned by George Bush. It also reflected the white reaction to black crime that has placed new emphasis on capital punishment and prisons that by making lockdowns and rock breaking routine do their best to humiliate inmates.[17]

■ ■ ■

Poor blacks are, of course, the ones who have suffered the most when the work-welfare-crime race card is played. But they are not the only ones to suffer in this atmosphere. The idea that blacks are a threat to the social order, no longer a deserving minority, has made it easier for whites to oppose the kinds of affirmative action programs that over the last two decades have helped middle-class blacks. From this point of view, as Andrew Hacker points out, affirmative action is simply a sophisticated version of welfare.[18]

In today's economy the competition for jobs and schooling is so fierce that it is not surprising that many whites feel threatened by affirmative action. A 1995 *Newsweek* poll showed that by a 79 to 14 percent margin whites opposed affirmative action in employment and college admissions. What the racial meanness of the nineties has done is increase these fears. The impulse behind affirmative action has always been a complex one, as Supreme Court Justice Harry Blackmun made clear in the *Bakke* case of 1978, when he declared, "In order to get beyond racism, we must first take account of race." Blackmun's point was that our past racial history had left blacks and other minorities at a disadvantage and that to remedy this disadvantage, we could not simply level the playing field. We had to do more. For Congress at that time it meant sanctioning programs that set aside places for minorities, and for the Supreme Court in the late seventies and early eighties it meant upholding plans in schools, government, and businesses that gave minorities group preferences.[19]

It was never an easy balance to maintain. Affirmative action goals could easily turn into quotas, and, especially in education, the sacrifices required by affirmative action fell on whites who were too young to have participated in legally sanctioned segregation. What has happened in the 1990s, however, is that the opposition to affirmative action has taken such a harsh and spiteful path that it has turned the debate over affirmative action from a search for difficult racial solutions to a winner-take-all battle for power.

In *The End of Racism* Dinesh D'Souza, a research fellow at the American Enterprise Institute, writes of the impact of affirmative action on business, "The cost of diversity is the cost of lowered standards across the board, so that companies end up with less able employees, poor teamwork, and reduced productivity." It is a description very similar to one that University of Texas law professor Lino Graglia gives when he talks about the affirmative action students admitted to colleges. "A frequently noted effect," he writes, "is virtually to guarantee that the preferentially admitted students are placed in schools for which they are greatly underqualified. It is as if professional baseball decided to 'advantage' an identifiable group of players at the beginning of their professional careers by placing them in a league at least one level above the one in which they could be expected to compete effectively." What unites these descriptions is not only their doubts about affirmative action. Just as important is their tone. In their patronizing view of affirmative action's recipients, they close the door on any serious discussion of the problems that affirmative action has attempted to deal with.[20]

For politicians, the affirmative action backlash of the nineties, legitimized in no small measure by thinking like D'Souza's and Graglia's, has been a powerful draw. In California, where in 1996 voters passed the state's anti–affirmative action Proposition 209, the California Civil Rights Initiative, by a 54-to-46 margin, Governor Peter Wilson was able to solidify his conservative base by his early support and fund raising for Proposition 209, and at the national level politicians have not hesitated to exploit the anti–affirmative action mood of the country. As the 1996 presidential campaign wound down, Bob Dole, who in his acceptance speech at the Republican National Convention made a point of proclaiming that his party was the party of Lincoln, delivered a blistering attack on affirmative action. "We cannot fight the evil of discrimination with more discrimination, because this leads to an endless cycle of bitterness," Dole declared in an October 28 speech in San Diego in which he went on to talk not only about the danger of quotas and preferences but to link support of affirmative action with our failure to end black unemployment and black crime.[21]

In the 1990s white politicians have, however, been spared, for the most part, from the actual dirty work of dismantling affirmative action. The Supreme Court has done that for them, and in the process sent a clearer message to blacks than any other institution that it is racial payback time. A century ago Justice Joseph Bradley, speaking for a Supreme Court that had just rendered the Civil Rights Act of 1875 unenforceable, declared, "When a man has emerged from slavery, and by the aid of beneficent legislation has shaken off the inseparable concomitants of that state, there must be some stage in the progress of his elevation when he takes the rank of mere citizen and ceases to be the special favorite of the laws." For the Supreme Court of the 1990s, a parallel view of our current history, accompanied by the notion that blacks are asking for affirmative action benefits they don't deserve, prevails, and the result is that just as the Supreme Court of the late nineteenth century stopped Reconstruction in its tracks, so the Supreme Court of the 1990s has reduced affirmative action to a vestige of what it was.[22]

How far the Court of the 1990s was prepared to retreat on affirmative action became apparent in 1995. In mid-June, in the case of *Adarand v. Pena*, the Court struck down a Department of Transportation order that set aside 10 percent of the money spent on federal highway projects for minority businesses. Speaking for a five-to-four majority, Justice Sandra Day O'Connor wrote, "We hold today that all racial classifications, imposed by whatever Federal, state, or local governmental actor, must be analyzed by a reviewing court under strict scrutiny. In other words such classifications are constitutional only if they are narrowly tailored measures that serve a compelling government interest." As recently as 1980 the Court had given the federal government exemption from this strict-scrutiny test, which has traditionally required proof of overt discrimination, on the grounds that constitutionally it had the "necessary latitude" to take more far-reaching initiatives. But in *Adarand* the Court not only reversed its own fifteen-year precedent, it set up a burden of proof virtually impossible to meet in the nineties, where it is the vestiges of discrimination, not overt discrimination, that is the problem for minorities.[23]

The plaintiff in *Adarand* was a white Colorado contractor who had lost a job building guard rails to a minority contractor despite submitting a lower bid. But the implications of *Adarand* went far beyond its specifics. In setting up a strict-scrutiny standard, the Court was in essence saying that whatever lingering effects past history might have on the ability of minority businesses to compete no longer mattered. The past was over as far as the Court was concerned. Minority businesses were on their own as far as future help from the government went.

Two weeks later the Court showed that its stance in *Adarand* was no fluke. In *Miller v. Johnson* it dealt affirmative action a second major setback when it held that a majority black district created to give blacks greater representation in Georgia was unconstitutional because it was drawn with race as the "predominant factor" and could not meet the test of strict scrutiny. Three years earlier in the controversial case of *Shaw v. Reno*, the Court had ruled that a North Carolina district drawn in order to increase black representation was so bizarre in shape that it constituted racial gerrymandering. But in *Miller v.*

Johnson, where the district in question would have given blacks, who are 27 percent of Georgia's population, a majority in three of the state's eleven congressional districts, the Court dropped the shape question entirely. It held that so long as race was the predominant factor motivating the drawing of an election district, a state needed to show that its actions were designed to provide a remedy for past discrimination, not merely increase current black representation.

The five-to-four decision, written by Justice Anthony Kennedy, was a setback for the Justice Department, which in the Bush and Clinton administrations had interpreted the 1982 amendments to the Voting Rights Act to mean that it should pursue the creation of minority election districts in states where minorities are underrepresented. But it is not only the Justice Department's bipartisan voting rights strategy that has been curtailed by *Miller. Miller* also throws into question the process by which since 1990 fourteen states have adopted redistricting plans that have doubled the number of congressional districts with black or Hispanic majorities from twenty-six to fifty-two. As Representative Cynthia McKinney, whose majority-black district was the focus of *Miller v. Johnson* sardonically remarked, the Court's ruling makes the "ultimate bleaching" of Congress much easier to bring about with all of the fifty-two minority districts now vulnerable in a way they were not before to suits by disgruntled white voters.[24]

The most dramatic racial retreat the Supreme Court of the 1990s has made is, however, in education. Although the Court has not ruled definitively in an affirmative action education case, instead contenting itself with letting stand a Fifth Circuit court ruling that says "the use of race to achieve a diverse student body cannot be a state interest compelling enough to meet the steep standard of strict scrutiny," it has ruled definitively with regard to school desegregation, and here it has more than lived up to former civil rights leader and one-time Georgia legislator Julian Bond's observation, "If you didn't know it was 1995, you'd swear it was 1895."[25]

In a 1991 case involving the Oklahoma City public schools, the Court showed how it was thinking when it lifted a thirty-year-old desegregation order on the grounds that it was residential segregation, motivated by private decision-making and economics, that was keeping Oklahoma City's public schools overwhelmingly black. Enough was enough, the Court said; the role played by state-sanctioned segregation in setting up the residential segregation that divided the city's schools into black and white no longer mattered.[26]

Four years later the Court showed just how far it was prepared to go in limiting desegregation remedies. In *Missouri v. Jenkins*, in a five-to-four decision written by Chief Justice William Rehnquist, the Court ruled unconstitutional a decision by a district judge ordering the state of Missouri to help pay for magnet schools designed to draw white students back into Kansas City's public schools. The district judge, the Court held, had exceeded his authority by authorizing taxes for a school desegregation plan that crossed district boundaries. The *Jenkins* decision left Kansas City authorities, whose magnet-school plan was designed for voluntary participation rather than required busing, nowhere to turn. The district did not have enough money or a sufficient racial mix to build workable magnet schools of its own. But even more important, at a time when 70 percent of the nation's black children attend schools that are segregated and only one in four children in the country's forty-seven largest school districts is white, the *Jenkins* decision sent a chilling message to educators trying to stop resegregation from getting worse. Forget it, the Court in effect told them. Even voluntary desegregation plans are illegal if they involve using tax dollars to get students to cross school district lines. Separate but equal schools, provided the state does not deliberately encourage such a policy, are tolerable.[27]

■ ■ ■

Thirty years ago, as white resistance to the civil rights movement escalated, it became clear that more than just legal remedies would be required to achieve racial equality. As Martin Luther King observed in his final book, "What is most needed is a coalition of Negroes and liberal whites that will work to make both major parties truly responsive to the needs of the poor." In the 1990s such a message, even when advanced by Georgia congressman and former Student Non-Violent Coordinating Committee chairman John Lewis, does not have the power it did when the civil rights movement was an important force in

American life. Far more influential is the notion that for blacks the only way to deal with the racial turn so much of white America has taken is to respond with comparable meanness.[28]

The change is epitomized by the role Louis Farrakhan played at the 1995 Million Man March. In 1994, when the Nation of Islam began planning for the march, it was to be a national "holy day of atonement and reconciliation" in which black men would pledge responsibility for themselves and their families. That is exactly what the day turned out to be for most of the middle-class and working-class men who went to Washington (an unpublished survey by two Howard University political scientists, Michael Frazier and Joseph McCormick, found that more than 71 percent of the participants claimed household incomes between $39,000 and $100,000 per year). The racial tone taken by Louis Farrakhan at the march was, however, very different. From the start it was dominated by spite. On the Friday before the march, he gave a preview of what was to come by making public an interview in which he called Jews "bloodsuckers," and then went on to say that as merchants Arabs, Koreans, and Vietnamese were no better than Jews in their relations with the black community.[29]

At the march itself Farrakhan continued in the same vein. In contrast to Martin Luther King, who thirty-two years earlier at the March on Washington had begun his "I have a dream" speech by describing Lincoln as "a great American, in whose symbolic shadow we stand," Farrakhan moved to the heart of his speech by describing

Lincoln as the man who "allegedly freed us" but who was really a racist at heart, opposed to the idea of blacks "having equal status with the whites of this nation." Like George Washington and Thomas Jefferson before him, what worried Lincoln, Farrakhan went on to say, was not the injustice of racism but the trouble blacks would pose for whites once they got their freedom. Farrakhan's point — and the reductive conclusion that went along with it — was unmistakable. The three presidents honored by the three greatest monuments in Washington were hypocrites, whose racial legacy was not in any way to be trusted by blacks. Blacks could only look on them with contempt and remember that what they represented was not an egalitarian tradition but the evil that undergirds the setup of America — "white supremacy."[30]

Farrakhan's sense that white America could only be understood in such racial terms paralleled the message sent by black pop culture when Nelson Mandela made his triumphal visit to America in 1990. Just before Mandela arrived, vendors began selling a line of T-shirts bearing his picture and a map of South Africa with the slogan "It's a black thing. You wouldn't understand." The Mandela T-shirts have become collector's items, but the slogan has lasted. Without Mandela's picture or a map of South Africa, "It's-a-black-thing. You-wouldn't-understand-it" T-shirts have become standard summer apparel for black kids across the country.[31]

Even more telling, the racial spite that underlies the slogan and seeks to put whites in their place has come to pervade a wide range of black culture in the nineties. For the working-class and middle-class blacks who go to colleges where whites are the majority, such feelings have increasingly turned out to be the norm. Several years ago Garry Trudeau lampooned where these feelings were leading in a highly publicized *Doonesbury* cartoon that showed a group of black students who had taken over a university building negotiating with the administration. When asked what they wanted, the students sent out a note demanding separate water fountains. The cartoon was funny, but the sensibility it spoke to is not. In 1994 at San Francisco State, it reached a peak when a controversy erupted over a Malcom X mural that appeared with an American flag, dollar signs, stars of David, and a skull and crossbones on its border. "We don't owe white folks an explanation," the mural's creator announced after protests arose when his work was publicly shown. The mural was an extreme case, but variations on it are not. As Ellis Cose notes in *The Rage of a Privileged Class*, the nineties have been a period in which black student groups have made a point of inviting campus speakers who they know will spew anti-white and, particularly, anti-Jewish invective in their talks. Indeed, even at colleges that aren't haunted by such direct confrontations, separate black dorms, separate black graduation committees, and separate black dining tables — all of which would be regarded as intolerable if whites asked for them — have become standard strategies for making racial exclusion routine.[32]

A similar animus has also come to shape the long-standing controversy over interracial adoption. The problem has become increasingly acute, as the proportion of black children waiting for adoption has risen to 67 percent of the total, while the proportion of black families seeking to adopt, 31 percent, is less than half that figure. But despite long-term studies showing that black children who grow up in white adoptive families do just as well as black children who grow up in black adoptive families, the small-but-powerful National Association of Black Social Workers has, even with changes in the law, managed to keep transracial adoptions to a minimum by insisting that "black men and women are the only people who can effectively teach black boys and girls about society's developed expectations and the racism inherent in them." For black children, the consequence has been much longer stays in institutions and much more difficulty in finally getting adopted than necessary; but just as troubling, as Harvard law professor Randall Kennedy argues, is the consequence for society: the perpetuation of "a rigid determinism according to which people of one race are thought simply incapable of fully loving people of another race."[33]

Meanwhile, causing the most bitter feelings of all, has been the rise of black bias crime. In his autobiography *Parallel Time, New York Times* editor Brent Staples describes how as a graduate student he made a point of stalking white people in order to frighten them. In a game he called Scatter the Pigeons, Staples would suddenly loom up before unsuspecting whites. "I became expert in the language of fear. Couples locked arms or reached for each other's hand when they saw me," Staples writes. "I felt a surge of power: these people were mine. I could do with them as I wished. If I'd been younger, with less to lose, I'd have robbed them, and it would have been easy." The kind of restraint Staples showed has not, however, been part of nineties culture. Animated by racial spite, black bias crimes have soared in recent years. In 1993 the Southern Poverty Law Center found that 46 percent of all the racially motivated killings that it tracked were committed by blacks, and across the country violent black crime, primarily motivated by racial spite, has made itself felt in a series of highly publicized incidents that have taken on a life of their own. In the 1992 Los Angeles riots, the savage beating of white truck driver Reginald Denny and the sight of rioters shouting "no pity for the white man" made the scapegoating that was part of the violence unmistakable. Two years later, the reaction by blacks to Colin Ferguson, the Long Island Rail Road gunman, who shot twenty-five white commuters and left a note explaining his racial anger, showed the same scapegoating at work. Instead of being seen as an embarrassment, Ferguson was given hero status by groups of blacks. When Louis Farrakhan, speaking at a New York rally a few weeks after the shooting, mentioned Ferguson's name, he drew an ovation, and the same reaction occurred in Washington when Nation of Islam speaker Khalid Muhammad told a Howard University audience, "I love Colin Ferguson."[34]

■   ■   ■

Surveying where all this racial meanness has left us, Henry Louis Gates, Jr., the chairman of Harvard's Afro-American Studies Department, in an essay written at the conclusion of O. J. Simpson's criminal trial, observed that we are caught up in a black-white discourse in which we only seem able to match accusation with counteraccusation, grievance with countergrievance. "It is a discourse in which O. J. Simpson is a suitable remedy for Rodney King and reductions in Medicaid are entertained as a suitable remedy for O. J. Simpson: a discourse in which everybody speaks of payback and nobody is paid," Gates wrote. A year later legal scholar Jeffrey Rosen, reviewing the Simpson trial for the *New Republic*, carried Gates's payback analysis still further. Defense attorney Johnnie Cochran's call for the jury to use its verdict to "send a message," Rosen noted, was rooted in the belief, gaining increasing respectability, that blacks should use their power as jurors to free other blacks, regardless of the evidence. And Jo-Ellan Dimitrius, the jury consultant who helped pick the pro-defense, predominantly black Simpson jury, had, Rosen pointed out, also helped choose the all-white jury that in 1992 acquitted the four police officers accused of beating Rodney King.[35]

Gates's and Rosen's analyses of the Simpson trial provide as good a description as we have of the ways in which the racial meanness of the nineties has trapped us. But just as important, they reflect how difficult it has become to find a way out of that trap. Thirty-four years ago, after defeating the efforts of Governor George Wallace to prevent two black students from enrolling in the University of Alabama, John Kennedy went on television to deliver a nationwide address. "If an American, because his skin is dark, cannot eat lunch in a restaurant open to the public, if he cannot send his children to the best public school available, if he cannot vote for the public officials who represent him," Kennedy asked, "then who among us would be content to have the color of his skin changed and stand in his place?"

Kennedy was explaining his actions in Alabama and at the same time preparing the way for the legislation that he would submit to Congress and that a year after his death would become the Civil Rights Act of 1964. But he was also doing something else that was unmistakable. In his role as president of the United States, he was apologizing for the nation's racial past, asserting, as he put it, that segregation was "an arbitrary indignity that no American in 1963 should have to endure, but many do." It was an apology that enhanced Kennedy's stature as a president. He was perceived as stronger, not weaker, for it. Three decades later, however, the racial meanness that surrounds us has not only made this kind of apology a liability for most white politicians, it has locked us into roles in which racial concession is taken as a sign of weakness. The payoff, especially in politics, comes from playing hardball, from making sure every racial encounter is treated as a symbolic clash of interests.[36]

5 Lifeboat Ethics and Immigration Fears

"IT LOOKS LIKE ROD-
ney King all over again," observed Ramona Ripston, the
executive director of the Southern California American
Civil Liberties Union. "The officers just beat these people
up." What Ripston was referring to was the videotape
made on the afternoon of April 1, 1996, by Los Angeles
television station KCAL of the beating of two illegal immigrants by Riverside County sheriff's deputies, after an
eighty-mile car chase in which the driver of the pickup
carrying the two immigrants and nineteen other illegals
sought to avoid capture.[1]

Although the beating with nightsticks was brutal and
one of the victims was a woman, two weeks later, at a
Riverside Law Enforcement Appreciation Rally, it was the
deputies who had done the beating who were being de-
fended and their victims who were the target of the rally
speakers' anger. By the start of May the controversy inten-
sified even more when immigration officials issued work

permits to sixteen of the immigrants involved in the chase so that they could remain in the country to testify in any future court case. On California talk shows and in letters to the editors, there was not only enormous sympathy for the situation the sheriff's deputies had found themselves in but a sense that they had dispensed needed justice. As the mayor of a nearby town observed of the fleeing immigrants, "These people are lawbreakers. What do they expect? They created the problem, they should expect the consequences. We're putting our police in a situation where they're afraid to do anything." What most infuriated those who supported the Riverside deputies, it was clear, were lenient penalties for entering the country illegally. A good beating, they all but stated, would teach a lesson the law could not.[2]

The anger that the Riverside beating controversy speaks to concerns more, however, than just too many of "them" coming across our borders. Also at work is a sense that the nation isn't making it economically and that taking in more people will make our problems even worse. As Democratic party pollster Mark Mellman put it, "Today the notion is that the pie is shrinking and that each new person who arrives not only takes a piece of the pie but takes it from me."[3]

The most dramatic example of such anti-immigration fears overwhelming all other considerations and changing the political landscape of a region occurred two years before the Riverside beatings. In the 1994 midterm elections in California, voters were presented with Proposition 187, an initiative designed to cut virtually all state aid, except for emergency hospital care, to illegal aliens. In a state in which government officials estimated the cost to taxpayers for illegal aliens and their American-born children at $3 billion annually — $1.1 billion in education, $950 million in health care, and $500 million each in welfare and prison costs — the questions raised by Proposition 187 were in themselves crucial. But as the debate over Proposition 187 heated up, the distinction it drew between legal and illegal immigrants became increasingly marginal. Long before the November elections the real intent of Proposition 187 was signaled by its supporters when they named it the SOS ("Save Our State") initiative.[4]

The literature handed out along with the initiative was even blunter in its appeals to resentment and its reluctance to concede that immigrants coming into the state were driven by a sense of desperation and a willingness to take almost any job. "While our own citizens and legal residents go wanting, those who choose to enter our country ILLEGALLY get royal treatment at the expense of the California tax payer," one ballot description read. Another hammered home the laziness of the newcomers. "Welfare, medical, and educational benefits are the magnets that draw ILLEGAL ALIENS," it declared. "WE CAN STOP THE ILLEGAL ALIEN INVASION NOW." Missing was any notion that today's immigrants might resemble those of the past in their character and ambition. As a television commercial argued, the only proper way for a struggling Californian to look on illegal immigrants was as leeches: "300,000 illegal immigrant children in public schools . . . and they keep coming. It's unfair when people like you are working hard," the voice-over in one of the governor's ads reminded voters.[5]

For Governor Pete Wilson, seemingly headed for defeat when the 1994 campaign began, a pro-Proposition 187 stance, combined with a platform that declared all Californians should be required to carry ID cards when applying for a job or a government benefit, was enough to provide the basis for a come-from-behind victory over popular Secretary of State Kathleen Brown. In 1993 Wilson's approval rating put him 23 points behind Brown, but by election time he had made up the difference with ads that featured black-and-white footage of hordes of Mexicans storming border check points and a voice-over in which he declared, "I'm suing to force the federal government to control the border. . . . Enough is enough." Wilson was able to strike a raw nerve, and in a state that voted for Proposition 187 by a three-to-two margin, it was not finally just anxious white voters who responded to his scare campaign. As a *Los Angeles Times* exit poll showed, Proposition 187 got 47 percent of the black vote, 47 percent of the Asian vote, and 23 percent of the Latino vote.[6]

Wilson was not, moreover, alone among California politicians in arguing that it was time to get tough with unwanted immigrants. Long before the 1994 elections, California officials at all levels had made a point of calling for tougher sanctions on immigrants. Senator Dianne Feinstein called for additional Border Patrol agents and a dollar-per-person border-crossing fee to pay for the additional agents. Senator Barbara Boxer advocated using the National Guard to help with Border Patrol work and increasing the penalties for the forgery of immigration documents. Even liberal politicians understood that in the California of the 1990s being called soft on immigration was fatal.[7]

As the 1990s have progressed, California's mood on immigration has become the nation's, even leading Congress to pass its own version of Proposition 187, a 1996 House bill that would allow states to deny public education to illegal immigrant children. The breadth of resentment that has made such a change possible was caught in 1993 by a Yankelovich poll which showed that 64 percent of the country think most immigrants enter the United States illegally; 64 percent believe they take jobs from Americans; and 59 percent believe they add to the crime problem. Time has not lessened the resentment. In a 1994 Times Mirror Center poll, 82 percent of those asked said that the United States should restrict immigration, and in a 1996 Roper poll, fewer than 6 percent of those surveyed said they approve of current immigration policy.[8]

The result is that we have crossed a threshold on what can be said in public about immigration. In Los Angeles during the 1993 debate over immigration the White Aryan Resistance distributed a flyer that showed a pregnant Mexican woman with a burrito for a placenta and carried a caption that announced, "Finally, an answer to the age old scientific mystery, 'How do Mexicans manage to reproduce so rapidly?'" In *Twilight: Los Angeles 1992*, her one-woman play about the Los Angeles riots, Anna Deavere Smith quotes Paul Parker, the chairman of the Free the LA Four Plus Defense Committee, saying of burning down Korean stores, "The Koreans was like the Jews in the day and we put them in check. You know, we got rid of all those Korean stores over there." Such open attacks on immigrants remain unacceptable, but in the 1990s they mark where the boundary lies. In California, Republican Assemblyman William Knight stirred up anger, even within his own party, but was able to get away with distributing a ditty, sent to him by a constituent, in which a new Mexican immigrant declares:

> Everything is mucho good
> Soon we own the neighborhood.
> We have a hobby. It's called breeding
> Welfare pay for baby feeding.

And on a much more serious level, archconservative Thomas Fleming, the editor of *Chronicles*, the Rockford Institute's monthly magazine, has not had to pay a political price for saying of current immigration, "More fruit pickers we do not need. Cut off the welfare payments, and we shall be surprised how many agricultural laborers are living right now in Chicago and New York."[9]

Several years ago, in an effort to portray the historical momentousness of the shift in our thinking on immigration, *American Heritage* magazine carried a cover on which the Statue of Liberty was shown with her torch hand pointing out to sea rather than lighting the way into New York Harbor. The magazine was being ironic, but increasingly in the nineties we are not. We are more and more at ease with the kind of nativism Pat Buchanan expressed on the campaign trail when he asked voters, "If we had to take a million immigrants in, say Zulus, next year, or Englishmen, and put them in Virginia, what group would be easier to assimilate and cause less problems for the people of Virginia?" The most thorough defense of Buchanan's "Zulu theory" may be found in Peter Brimelow's 1995 polemic, *Alien Nation: Common Sense about America's Immigration Disaster*. In a book hauntingly reminiscent of Lothrop Stoddard's 1920 study, *The Rising Tide of Color*, which contended that the white race was in danger of being "swamped by the triumphant colored races, who will obliterate the white man by elimination or absorption," the English-born Brimelow, a senior editor at *Forbes*, warns that the current mass immigration from predominantly non-European countries threatens not only the "racial hegemony of white Americans" but the ethnic balance responsible for our social cohesion as a nation. He even provides a "pincer chart" showing America's white population being squeezed between the pincers of blacks and Asians, on the one hand, and the Hispanics, on the other. Continued unchecked immigration, Brimelow argues, promises to put America in the position faced by the Western Roman Empire during the fifth century, when it was overrun by the Germanic tribes of Europe.[10]

In his worry over *who* is coming to America, Peter

Brimelow is, however, far from the odd intellectual out these days. A year before the publication of *Alien Nation*, John O'Sullivan, a *National Review* editor, in an essay entitled "America's Identity Crisis," expressed much the same fear: "When immigrants arrive in large numbers from cultures that stress different rules and even disregard those embodied in American culture, this reduces the status of American culture. It becomes merely 'Anglo' culture, whose rules, standards, and conventions are thought to be alien to non-Anglo citizens and hence cannot be 'imposed' on them." It is a view also held, in a subtler way, by diplomatic historian George Kennan. In his 1996 collection of essays, *At a Century's Ending*, he warns in language not unlike Brimelow's that we are headed for trouble if we fail "to control the immigration into our midst of great masses of people of wholly different cultural and political traditions."[11]

Mainstream politicians at the national level cannot openly claim to be guided by such advice. But they have found ways to make it clear to voters that they are thinking along such lines. During the 1996 presidential campaign, the Dole and Clinton immigration ads both took as their starting point the idea that toughness on immigration was essential and that voters saw immigrants as a threat. In a Republican ad entitled "More," immigrants were shown sneaking into the country from Mexico, and the Clinton administration was charged with not doing enough to stop them. "You spend $5.5 billion to support illegals," the ad charged. "Tell President Clinton: stop giving illegal

benefits to illegals. End wasteful Washington spending."
The National Democratic Committee's rejoinder was just
as harsh. Its ad began by refuting the Republicans' charges,
but lest it be taken as a pro-immigration ad, it quickly
switched to a negative portrayal of immigrants. As in the
Republican ad, they were shown as dark, swarthy figures
trying to enter the country illegally. The difference was
that in the Democrats' ad they didn't make it. They were
nabbed by the Border Patrol (actually put in handcuffs),
and the ad pointed out that under the Clinton administration the Border Patrol had been increased by 40 percent
and deportations were at record numbers.[12]

For politicians without such advertising budgets at
their disposal, it has been possible to convey the same resentments through legislative proposals that even when
they don't succeed, make it clear that the welcome mat is
no longer out for newcomers. Calls for a fence along our
border with Mexico, once parodied by the *New York Times*
in an article that facetiously discussed the cost of land-
scaping the fence with shrubs and flowers, have come to
command attention for no other reason than the message
they send. The same is true for proposals to make being
born on American soil no longer a guarantee of citizenship
(if your parents are illegal aliens) and to elevate English to
the status of our official language. Neither proposal is likely
to have much direct impact anytime soon. The first would
require a constitutional amendment. The second is gratuitous at a time when English-language classes are overcrowded with immigrants. But like the idea of a border

fence, the point is the underlying message. The first proposal tells potential immigrants that we don't think of you as we did of immigrants in the past. The second turns English into a weapon for fighting diversity, for making those who were once outsiders continue to feel like outsiders.[13]

■ ■ ■

We have come a long way in a short time from being the nation that as recently as 1984 felt the social confidence to laugh at the melting-pot humor in the film *Moscow on the Hudson*, in which Robin Williams, playing a Russian refugee, finds himself sheltered by a black family, aided by a Cuban lawyer, and in love with a recent Italian immigrant. These days, even when we joke about immigration, as the *Chicago Tribune*'s Mike Royko tried to do in a 1996 column parodying Pat Buchanan by describing Mexico as a "useless country" that we should seize "before its entire population sneaks across the border," it is hard to get away from a meanness that surfaces whenever immigration is in the air. The longer Royko talked about Mexico as a country that was such a mess because "it is run by Mexicans who clearly have established that they don't know what they are doing," the harder it got to tell if Buchanan was his target or he was using his parody to vent his own resentments about immigration from south of the border.[14]

That there would ever be an immigration backlash was unforeseen by those who fought to liberalize America's immigration laws three decades ago. In 1965, when the Immigration and Nationality Act Amendments responsible for our current mass immigration were enacted, the assumption on the part of the amendments' supporters was that a new era of social justice was beginning. For the previous forty-one years immigration to America had been reduced dramatically by the Johnson-Reed Act of 1924. Between 1925 and 1965 just 178,000 people entered the country annually. Passed at a time when anti-immigration fever was running high, the 1924 act set a yearly limit of 150,000 on immigrants from outside the Western Hemisphere and then divided them into quotas based on each country's share of the total American population of 1920. The national-origins system favored the descendants of those who had been here the longest, the British and northern Europeans.

A *Los Angeles Times* headline hailing the 1924 law as a "Nordic Victory" was not off the mark. Chinese immigrants, as a result of extensions of the Chinese Exclusion Act of 1882, which would not be repealed until 1943, were already barred, and Japanese, through a provision of the 1924 act that excluded immigrants who were ineligible to become citizens, were also effectively kept out. The immigration tide that from 1880 to 1920 had brought 23.5 million people to America was over. Between 1920 and 1930 immigration dropped to just over 4 million. In the Depression years of the 1930s it was barely half a million, and in the 1940s, despite special legislation that paved the way for hundreds of thousands of displaced World War II victims to come to America, the number of immigrants was only a million.

The McCarran-Walter Immigration and Nationality Act of 1952 did little to change this pattern. Passed over the veto of President Harry Truman, who wanted a more liberal immigration law, the McCarran-Walter Act retained most of the quota preferences of 1924. Asians could now immigrate, but their numbers, like those of southern Europeans, were kept low. From 1951 to 1960 only 2.5 million immigrants came to the United States.

The Immigration and Nationality Act Amendments of 1965 were designed to undo this pattern. Coming at the peak of the civil rights revolution, the amendments reflected the social optimism of the Johnson administration and the views of a coalition of Jews, Catholics, and liberals that had fought for years against the biases of the 1924 law. The new amendments limited immigration from Western Hemisphere countries for the first time, but in every other respect the 1965 amendments were revolutionary. The new law abandoned all efforts to distinguish among immigrants on the basis of their race or their historical link to America. Up to 20,000 people could come in any year from a single nation. The dominating principle was now family reunification. Eighty percent of the numerically limited visas were for close relatives of American citizens or residents.[15]

In proposing the legislation that would eventually become the Immigration and Nationality Act Amendments of 1965, President Kennedy in an open letter to the House and Senate leadership emphasized the importance of doing away with the old quota system. "It neither satisfies a national need nor accomplishes an international purpose," he declared. "In an age of interdependence among nations, such a system is an anachronism, for it discriminates among applicants for admission to the United States on the basis of accident of birth." Two years later, at the Liberty Island signing ceremony for the bill, Lyndon Johnson returned to the same themes in words reminiscent of those he had used in signing the Voting Rights Act months earlier. The new immigration bill, the president insisted, repairs "a deep and painful flaw in the fabric of American justice. It corrects a cruel and enduring wrong in the conduct of the American nation."[16]

For the president and the immigration bill's supporters, there was, however, a second reason for optimism as well. They had, they believed, achieved a legislative victory that would not cause them political problems in the future. "The bill that we sign today is not a revolutionary bill," Johnson emphasized. "It does not affect the lives of millions. It will not reshape the structure of our daily lives, or really add importantly to either our wealth or power." Senator Edward Kennedy, the bill's floor manager, was equally sanguine about its future. "Our cities will not be flooded with a million immigrants annually. Under the proposed bill the present level of immigration remains substantially the same," he told critics. His brother Robert, as attorney general, was also upbeat, assuring a House subcommittee worried over the potential influx of Asian immigrants, that their number "would be approximately five thousand a year" at the start and then drop to a much lower figure.[17]

■   ■   ■

What the Johnson administration and the Kennedys failed to anticipate were the consequences of a loophole in the 1965 law that when limits were exceeded allowed the parents, spouses, and minor children of any adult American citizen to enter the country without being subject to numerical restrictions. Their calculations were based on the expected continuation of the earlier European patterns of immigration. But as Asian and Latin immigrants with large extended families replaced Europeans, the immigration multiplier — the number of admittances attributable to one immigrant — rose dramatically. The fifth preference in the 1965 law, which placed brothers and sisters high on the quota list, accelerated the process still more. Between 1971 and 1980, 4.5 million immigrants were admitted to the United States. In the 1980s the numbers increased still more by the amnesty granted in 1986 to 2.7 million illegal immigrants already living in the United States, climbed to a peak they had not reached since the turn of the century, and since then our current immigration rate of approximately a million immigrants per year has become the norm. By 2050, fueled by an immigration policy that has added 30 million immigrants and their descendents since 1970, America's population should reach 394 million, just 52.8 percent of whom will be non-Hispanic whites.[18]

It was not, however, only the size and makeup of future immigration that the supporters of the 1965 law miscalculated. In the midst of the prosperous 1960s, when the civil rights movement seemed as if it just might succeed, they also failed to anticipate the trouble that large-scale immigration would pose as jobs became scarce and America became an increasingly multiracial society. In 1995, as moves to restrict immigration bogged down in the House of Representatives, thirty-five congressmen wrote a public letter to Newt Gingrich, warning that current levels of immigration have "resulted in overcrowded schools and hospitals, scarce employment, inadequate housing and a deteriorating standard of living, as well as an undue burden on state and local governments." The congressmen were not engaging in hyperbole. At a time when AFDC payments of $25 billion per year have been a driving force behind Congress's decision to abandon the federal welfare system that has been in place since the New Deal, the cost to taxpayers for immigration has risen to $16 billion annually, according to immigration expert George Borjas of Harvard's John F. Kennedy School of Government. To make matters worse, the burdens of immigration have not fallen evenly across American society; those vulnerable to technological change and those at the bottom of the economic ladder have paid a higher price for immigration than anyone else.[19]

The problems begin with the geographic concentration of immigration. Seventy-nine percent of America's recent legal immigrants have settled in seven states —

California, New York, Florida, Illinois, New Jersey, Arizona, and Texas — with 40 percent of this group living in southern California. Illegal immigrants have followed the same pattern, with the result that the states paying the most for services to legal immigrants are also paying the most for illegals. The bill for the latter has been enormous. Educating 641,000 illegal immigrant children costs the seven states $3.1 billion annually. For Medicaid the cost is $422 million annually. For illegal immigrants in prisons, the cost is $471 million per year. Nor is there a way for the states to get back all the money they pay. In 1996 California's governor, Pete Wilson, sued the federal government for failing to reimburse his state for the cost of imprisoning undocumented aliens convicted of felonies. But his suit was largely a political gesture. If Washington repaid California for all it spent to imprison illegal aliens, there would be no money in the fund Congress appropriated for this purpose to pay any other state.[20]

Among those living in the high-density immigration states who are mobile enough to leave and find work elsewhere, there has been a significant outmigration in the nineties to parts of the country where the population has remained stable. For most people, however, roots are not that easy to pull up, and the result is that the immigration wave of the last two decades has created its own anti-immigration constituency, more than willing to give its approval to any measure it believes will limit the power of newcomers.[21]

At the core of this constituency are high-tech workers,

who since the start of the decade have become vulnerable to changes in the immigration law made during the Bush administration that allow companies to import foreign engineers and computer operators and pay them salaries that, in areas like Silicon Valley in California, have been averaging $7,000 a year less than what American-born workers with comparable training and education are paid. The new *technobraceros*, as they are called by their critics, have led one anti-immigrant group, Californians for Population Stabilization, to sue Hewlett-Packard of Palo Alto for unfair hiring practices, and in the East former IBM computer operator Lawrence Richards has formed the Software Professionals Political Action Committee. For the high-tech American workers, nothing, however, has changed the sense of being under siege and facing a situation in which, as one computer operator put it, "companies can get away with hiring at slave wages."[22]

Among union workers trying to hold on to blue-collar jobs that pay decent wages, a similar situation prevails. In 1979 United Farm Workers president Cesar Chavez complained to the Carter administration of the use California growers were making of illegal aliens. "The companies have to depend on the importation of people from Mexico. That is what has kept farm workers from organizing in the past," Chavez insisted. In the 1990s Chavez's complaint is one that may be applied across the country. In southern Florida the construction industry, which once paid middle-class wages and benefits, has become a low-wage industry as a result of the advantage contractors have taken of a steady influx of Cuban, Nicaraguan, and Haitian labor. In the West the meatpacking industry has undergone a similar transition in company after company through the use of Laotian, Vietnamese, and Mexican workers, and in California, drywallers, who were once represented by the carpenters' union, have seen their wages cut in half as a result of the ability of contractors to hire workers from Mexico. Where possible the unions have fought back, but even when they have won victories, what haven't gone away are the feelings of resentment that led American workers at a Midwest packing plant to post "Go Home!" picket signs around the trailer homes of new foreign workers who had just been hired.[23]

For blacks, especially those struggling to find entry-level jobs, the impact of immigration has been, if anything, more extreme. More than a century ago Frederick Douglass wrote about the impact of European immigration on ex-slaves like himself: "Our old employments by which we have been accustomed to gaining a livelihood are gradually slipping from our hands. Every hour sees us elbowed out of some employment to make room for some newly arrived emigrant." In the 1990s it is immigrants from Latin America and Asia who have taken the place of Europeans in elbowing out blacks in the competition for entry-level jobs. The reasons for this displacement — how much of it is due to the end of traditional factory work and how much of it is due to the unwillingness of blacks to take low-paying jobs — are much debated these days. But what is not in dispute is that the displacement has taken place and is increasing. In his 1996 study of Chicago, *When Work Disappears*, sociologist William Julius Wilson found more and more employers willing to speak openly about their belief that the new immigrants were better workers than inner-city blacks, and in his 1996 study of New York, *Still the Promised City?* UCLA professor Roger Waldinger not only found similar employer preferences operating but also an immigrant entry-level job network that time and again assured newcomers would be hired before blacks. As if this were not enough, in the competition for increasingly scarce affirmative action slots, black workers have also lost power to new immigrants. Originally conceived as a way of compensating for the vestiges of discrimination, such as poor education and inadequate job training, that civil rights law could not make up for, affirmative action has over the last twenty years been transformed into a leg up for women and for anyone who qualifies as a minority, including immigrants who were never in America when Jim Crow laws prevailed across the South. Since 1970 black Americans have gone from two-thirds of the affirmative action candidates to fewer than half.[24]

For blacks, 58 percent of whom believe, according to a 1996 Yankelovich–*New Yorker* survey, that conditions are getting harder for them, the increase in competition comes at the worst possible time. In California, where blacks have clashed with Latinos over city council seats in Los Angeles and with Asians over admission to Berkeley, the 47 percent of black voters who favored Proposition 187 was no fluke. That vote resulted from the same frustration that prompted Terry Anderson, a black board member of the Diversity Coalition for an Immigration Moratorium, to complain in a recent *Los Angeles Times* op ed, "Black people want to work. But the jobs they used to have paying $5 to $7 an hour for unskilled labor now go to immigrants for $3 an hour.... It's a culture clash. If you speak up, you're called a racist."[25]

■ ■ ■

Such ongoing resentment, linked as it is to real economic hardship, guarantees that the current immigration backlash will rest on a solid base for some time to come. But more than that, it guarantees support for a politics of spite in which our substitute for keeping immigrants out of the country is to make life as difficult as possible for those who are here, hoping that somehow they will either cease making demands or give up and deport themselves. *New York Times* columnist William Safire has described this strategy as one based on the belief we can "make 'em so miserable that they leave the country," and certainly we are no stranger to this ploy. As immigration historian John Higham argued several years ago, "We are now at the same point things were in 1912 with regard to that earlier wave of immigration. If Congress had acted earlier in the twentieth century, it would have diffused the pressure. But instead of getting a rational and equitable policy of regulation, what we finally got was a demeaning and racist policy."[26]

Our own version of such a policy came very close to

being embodied in the 1996 immigration bill that passed Congress just a month before the November elections. Only last-minute pressure from the administration removed from the bill provisions that would have barred legal immigrants with AIDS from access to federally financed health programs, deported other legal immigrants who had used certain public benefits for more than twelve months during their first seven years in the country, and required any legal immigrant wanting to bring a parent, a sibling, or an adult child into the country to have an income of double the poverty level.[27]

In the welfare bill that the president signed at the end of the summer of 1996, there was, however, no mistaking the animus toward immigrants. They were, along with the poor, the bill's prime targets. A minor concern during most of the debate over the welfare act, its immigrant provisions were anything but that in their final form. In requiring that in the future legal immigrants who are not citizens shall, for their first five years in the country, be ineligible for most federal benefits and social services, the welfare act doesn't just single out immigrants for different treatment. It places them in a separate-but-unequal category where they have the economic status of nonpersons — or, more precisely, illegal aliens. "There must be some distinction between citizens and noncitizens," Texas congressman Lamar Smith argued in defending the immigration provision of the welfare act. But with most new immigrants unable to become citizens on entering the country — the basic requirement, unless a special provision is made, is five years of continuous residency — what is really embodied in the immigration sections of the 1996 welfare act is not a defense of citizenship but its opposite: a defense of making becoming a citizen an ordeal. You are, the act tells new immigrants, the one group in our society who has no official claim on us, whom we feel free to bar from public assistance.[28]

This is the kind of message immigrants have heard for most of the decade, but coming as it does in the form of national legislation, it carries a different resonance. There is no mistaking its authority. Like the immigration quotas of the 1920s, what the immigration provisions of the welfare reform act of 1996 do is close the gap between scapegoating and official policy. In them there is no pretense that we only want to punish those who are here illegally and have evaded the law. The target is clear: immigrants who play by the rules.

6 Sexual Warfare and the Post-Liberated Man

In 1993 THE MAKERS of Brut fragrance launched a $10 million ad campaign based on the three-word slogan "Men Are Back." The slogan was not just a lucky guess about what men might like to hear. Behind it lay a Yankelovich survey in which 80 percent of the men polled said they would rather be movie tough guy Clint Eastwood than long-haired rocker Michael Bolton.

But the "Men Are Back" ad campaign proclaimed more than just the return of a man's man, who, as the sexy female voice-over of the Brut commercial told viewers, "doesn't like power breakfasts" and will "take a pass on poetry." The real appeal of the commercial depended on the implicit assertions about male sexuality that it made and with which it expected men to identify. In its visual image of a rugged man who knew himself and followed his own instincts, the Brut commercial supplied the answer to its own unstated question, Where are men back from?

Men, the commercial argued by implication, had lost their true selves. Women, specifically feminism, had done this to them. Real men — Brut men — were concerned with what had happened to their gender. They were, accordingly, not about to accommodate themselves to anyone else's idea of male behavior except their own.[1]

In a year in which a Gallup poll showed that nearly half the men in the country believed that the women's movement had made their lives harder, the Brut commercial struck a nerve. But even more, it captured the premises on which the Post-Liberated Man of the nineties, the titular successor of the Liberated Man of the seventies and eighties, has become the protagonist in a sexual culture war in which taking on contemporary feminism has unleashed an anger and meanness that leave little room for anything else. From Rush Limbaugh talking on the radio about "feminazis" to Arno Strine, the narrator of Nicholson Baker's best-selling novel *The Fermata*, using his magical powers to freeze women in time (literally stop history) and then undress them without their knowing it, the men engaged in this sexual culture war have moved far beyond what at the start of the decade feminist journalist Susan Faludi called male backlash.[2]

The willingness of so many men in the 1990s to get involved in this culture war has political as well as personal roots. The "angry white man" who sees himself pushed aside by affirmative action programs that favor women and minorities captured public attention during the 1994 midterm elections, when, in the biggest gender gap ever recorded in congressional history, 54 percent of all men and 62 percent of white men responded to the Contract with America by voting Republican. For men, especially white men, the resentments that the Contract fed off were an easy sell. Since the 1970s men's wages have been in decline, and for those brought up with the idea that the man of the family is also the breadwinner, the last two decades have been particularly bitter.[3]

In a period in which women's hourly wages have been rising and their share of executive and managerial jobs has increased, it is not, however, just the feeling of being displaced that has made men resentful. Men have come to see themselves on the losing end of a series of symbolic public gender battles. They are the ones the Antioch College Sex Codes are designed to put in their place. They are the ones the "Thelma and Louise Still Live" bumper stickers warn against. How much things have changed became clear with the notorious Lorena Bobbitt case of 1994, in which a Virginia jury accepted her claim that she was a victim of sexual abuse and refused to convict her of a crime for cutting off her husband's penis and throwing it in a field. The decision itself was shocking, but what was most telling for men was the reaction of women to the trial. The jokes, the cheering, the "Lorena Bobbitt for Surgeon General" buttons left no doubt that for many women what the jury's verdict really said was that here was a man who at last got what he had coming to him. As social critic Barbara Ehrenreich put it in her essay "Feminism Confronts Bobbittry," "If a fellow insists on using his penis as a weapon,

I say that, one way or another, he ought to be swiftly disarmed."[4]

■   ■   ■

In a *Playboy* column published at the end of 1994, humorist Cynthia Heimel conceded that a trend was at work. "Male bashing is everywhere," she observed. "TV sitcoms exist only to make men look ridiculous. In comedy clubs, women get big laughs tearing men to shreds." Heimel's advice to men was to remember how much real power they had and keep their situation in perspective. In the midst of a shaky economy and a social milieu in which even the president cannot shield himself from sexual harassment charges, the last thing men have found reassuring, however, is the position they occupy. In this context a sexual culture war that takes as its starting point an attack on feminism that questions both its integrity and the motives of its leadership has, like the Brut commercial, come as welcome relief for men.[5]

On the right, nobody has been more deeply engaged in this culture war than Rush Limbaugh, who, with a talk show that runs on 648 stations and pulls in 20 million listeners at least once a week, has made "feminazi" part of the national vocabulary. For Limbaugh, "Feminism was established so that unattractive women could have easier access to the mainstream of society." That, he concedes, is an ugly thing to say. "But the truth is the truth. And it needs to be heard." In Limbaugh's case it is also a starting point that allows him to frame his larger analysis of feminism on the premise that its most dearly held ideas are cover-ups and compensations for baser feelings. Given the number of unattractive women that he finds in feminism, it is only natural to Limbaugh that it is "basically anti-male" and that its leaders want "to make the case that any expression of interest by a man in a woman is harassment." It is enough to make Limbaugh so exasperated that in the middle of his essay "The Latest from the Feminist Front" he takes time out to lecture feminists on the facts of life. "It's normal for boys to pursue girls. It's natural for men to pursue women," he reminds them.[6]

Limbaugh knows that feminists don't need to be told about the facts of life, but doing so allows him to drive home his main point about feminism's leaders: these are women so ugly and sour that for all practical purposes they have forgotten what sexual joy is about. It is also a point that leads logically to his explanation for why feminists have put such an emphasis on lesbianism and "special rights for homosexuals." What is driving them to such "an extreme left-wing political agenda" is not, after all, egalitarianism but, it follows, self-interest and fondness for their own kind.[7]

From Limbaugh's perspective it also follows that what these "manhaters" really want is not equality with men but a different kind of society. "They are on a mission to change the fundamental relationship between the sexes," he writes. "They are at war with traditional American values and fundamental institutions such as marriage and the American family." For Limbaugh, it is not spiteful to call the most radical of these feminists "feminazis," for their goal, he believes, is a society in which men are dominated by women like them.[8]

The final sign of their insincerity lies, as far as he is concerned, with their stance on abortion. What is driving them, he argues, is not concern over unwanted children coming into the world but a desire for power. These are women who don't need men in order to be happy, and they certainly don't want men exercising control over them. Hence their pro-abortion position: "Abortion is the ultimate symbol of women's emancipation from the power and influence of men. With men being precluded from the ultimate decision-making process regarding the future of life in the womb, they are reduced to their proper, inferior role. Nothing matters but me, says the feminazi." For Limbaugh, this attitude is the final proof of the falseness of contemporary feminism and the reason its advocates should be viewed with contempt. That these same pro-abortion women are also in favor of welfare only shows the lengths to which they will go to advance a social policy that allows women to live without men.[9]

There is, Limbaugh concludes in his essay "Feminism and the Culture War," no making peace with such women. The only concession he is willing to offer is a facetious one concerning feminists in combat. An Amazon cavalry division with fifty-two battalions, one for every week of the year, would, he believes, be a good idea. It would give the country a combat-ready battalion of Amazons with PMS always available for battle with the enemy.[10]

It is not, however, only the conservative right that has attacked the integrity of feminism in the nineties. From the liberal left, an in many ways more damaging attack has been mounted by Warren Farrell, who in 1975 became a poster boy for feminism with his book *The Liberated Man* and then in 1993 sharply reversed course with *The Myth of Male Power*, in which he argued that over the last two decades men have allowed themselves to be silenced by a women's movement which is scornful of their problems.

Like Limbaugh, Farrell's point is that feminism has been less than honest about its intentions. In his case, however, the criticism is delivered from an insider's perspective. For three years Farrell served on the board of directors of the National Organization for Women (NOW), and for an even longer time he made his living lecturing primarily to women on gender issues. It was, Farrell acknowledges, a life he liked, and in the process of lecturing, he fell into the habit of adopting a feminist perspective. "When women criticized men, I called it 'insight,' 'assertiveness,' 'women's liberation,' 'independence,' or 'high self-esteem,'" he writes. "When men criticized women, I called it 'sexism,' 'male chauvinism,' 'defensiveness,' 'rationalizing,' and 'backlash.'" It all went well, Farrell goes on to say, until he became aware of his own biases and began to take a more evenhanded approach. The result was a disaster. "Almost overnight my standing ovations disintegrated. After each speaking engagement, I was no longer receiving three or four new requests to speak. My financial security was drying up." Feminists, Farrell found, did not want to hear both sides of the issue.[11]

In *The Myth of Male Power*, Farrell's point is that what he found out personally from dealing with feminists is also intellectually true of feminism. The movement lacks a basic honesty, and in the eighties and nineties, it has not had to own up to that fact. What this has meant in the picture feminism presents of the world, Farrell argues is, "Feminism suggested that God might be a 'She' but not that the devil might also be a 'she.' Feminism articulated the shadow side of men and the light side of women. It neglected the shadow side of women and the light side of men." For men, the consequences of this intellectual assault by feminism, Farrell concludes, have been nothing short of disastrous, and in a critical image as biting as any Limbaugh has offered up on radio, Farrell finishes off his analysis by declaring that feminism has turned out to play a role analogous to what "bacteria is to water."[12]

With such attacks on the integrity of feminism, it has become safe for those in the mainstream to dismiss all but the blandest forms of feminist thinking. Over the course of the nineties it has actually become easier, as the case of Vice President Dan Quayle's famous 1992 Murphy Brown speech shows, to treat feminism as morally suspect. In 1992, when Quayle attacked the television sitcom *Murphy Brown* for advocating a feminism "mocking the importance of fathers" because its lead character, played by Candace Bergen, opted to have a baby out of wedlock, he was immediately and sharply criticized for going out of his way to score political points. But since then Quayle's speech has come to be hailed as a classic defense of family values, while what has been forgotten is how derisive the speech was of the complex array of feminist issues Murphy Brown struggled with in deciding whether her age, her career, and her temperament would let her be a good mother.[13]

■ ■ ■

No less a casualty of the assault on feminism has been the ideal of the Liberated Man. The two were linked from the start. What gave credibility to the Liberated Man who sought to adapt himself to the women's needs feminism articulated was the credibility of feminism. When, for instance, men put themselves in women's and feminism's shoes, as they did in the 1980s in such changing-places films as *Mr. Mom* and *Tootsie*, they inevitably underwent internal change and became more liberated in their thinking. What the sexual culture war of the 1990s has done is reverse this process. These days the public figures — radio talk-show host Howard Stern and basketball player Dennis Rodman — who have made a point of going in drag and presumably changing places with women — are men who have been calculatedly up-front about their chauvinism and their interest in sexual scoring. As feminism has become more suspect, so has the Liberated Man. Especially in the literature of the sexual culture war, men can't find enough ways to express their contempt for their past "liberated" selves.

The direction this contempt would take was foreshadowed at the turn of the decade by poet Robert Bly in his 1990 bestseller *Iron John*. The book is a reworking of the 1820 Grimm's fairy tale of Iron John, a wild man who lives in the woods and is responsible for initiating a king's son into adult life. Bly believes that men still need an Iron John; in his book and in the all-male gathering ceremonies he led at that time, he tried to show how men might repeat the Iron John experience. But just as important to Bly is what happens to men who don't find an Iron John in their lives. In his book he never discusses feminism per se, and he never speaks of the Liberated Man. There is, however, no mistaking — as Susan Faludi, among other feminist critics, has noted — the contempt Bly has for what feminism and its supporters have done to the so-called Liberated Man.[14]

The contempt begins with Bly's summary of the last two decades of men's history. "The male in the past twenty years has become more thoughtful, more gentle," Bly writes. "But by this process he has not become more free. He's a nice boy who pleases not only his mother but also the young woman he is living with." Faced with the charge that he is too wild, this soft man has, Bly argues, only one response: mea culpa. "If his wife or girlfriend, furious, shouts that he is 'chauvinist,' a 'sexist,' a 'man,' he doesn't fight back, but just takes it. He opens his shirt so that she can see more clearly where to put the lances," Bly observes. "He feels, as he absorbs attacks, that he is doing the brave and advanced thing."[15]

Four years later essayist Lance Morrow took these same ideas and made them central to his *Time* magazine Valentine's Day cover story, "Men, Are They Really That Bad?" In Morrow's story there is, however, no hinting at the harm done by feminism. As the rhetorical question of his title and the exaggerated *Time* cover of a pig dressed up in a suit indicated, Morrow did not believe men were really bad. In his eyes what was really bad was the feminist vision of men, which had turned them into "the Germans of gender."[16]

In his essay, Morrow argues that the extremist vision of feminism has come to carry the day. It no longer represents the views of a small sect. "The overt man bashing of recent years has now refined itself into a certain atmospheric snideness — has settled down to a vague male aversion, as if masculinity were a bad smell in the room." Taking as his prime example Joyce Carol Oates's 1993 bestseller *Foxfire*, which celebrates the leader of a girl gang that beats up men as a way of getting social justice, Morrow contends that feminism has reached a point where it also has a gang mentality. "The assumption is that men are fair game," he writes. "Any man insulting is retributive: a payback for the years, the centuries of male domination and oppression. And for the continuing awfulness of man." The result is the triumph of what Morrow labels "a technique of gender slur that might be called Worst Case Synecdoche: All men are assumed to be as bad as the very worst among them. The rapist is Everyman."[17]

How can a man who wants to be caring respond

positively to such a sexual situation? Morrow's answer is that he cannot, and it is here that his essay makes its harshest and most contemptuous judgments. The men who take the "appease-the-sisters" approach to feminism are, he believes, simply giving in to their own ruin. There is no way to sympathize with them. What they have done — in contrast to the Brut man — is unman themselves. They have, he concludes, become "the descendants of the ancient priests of Cybele, who as part of their initiation would castrate themselves and sling their testicles into the earth mother's pine tree."[18]

Two months later, in an *Esquire* essay titled, "Post-Sensitive Man Is Coming," which acknowledged the importance of Morrow's piece, former *Esquire* ethics editor Harry Stein took the attack on the Liberated Man as far as it could go. Bly and Morrow had been concerned with blaming feminism for the Liberated Man. Stein did not deny that link, nor did he mince words about the venom that he felt contemporary feminism had inflicted on the culture. As he observed of the Bobbitt case, "Who could have imagined that seemingly reasonable women would one day go around high-fiving in the streets after the acquittal of a woman who'd cut off her husband's penis, taking the verdict as not merely one horrific wrong having neutralized another but as poetic justice itself?"[19]

But for Stein what was crucial was the role the Liberated Man, or, as he called him, the Sensitive Man, had played in turning himself into "basically a woman with a penis." It is this weakness on the part of the Liberated Man that allows Stein to feel justified in speaking of him with such contempt. "The sorry truth is that for a full generation men have been the willing cohorts in a screwy bit of social engineering — the fabrication of a more sensitive, tolerant, giving, *pliable* species of male," he writes. "It's what we thought women wanted. After all, this new improved man . . . definitely wasn't any guy's invention."[20]

"So here's the ugly truth: We let it happen," Stein goes on to add, "because, finally, throughout time and space, most of us have always taken our emotional clues from women." In his own case, Stein admits, he was just as bad as every other man. He became liberated in order to score with women. "In my own milieu the right gender politics soon became almost essential to getting laid — the good-guy's version of the strut." Women were angry, and he and other men like him were more than willing to meet them on their own terms. "We were ready to plead guilty in retrospect (and in theory), to all manner of transgressions — emotional, moral, intellectual," he confesses. "All we wanted was to be told we were okay."[21]

The upshot, Stein concludes, has been a revolt by formerly sensitive or liberated men like himself. "Suddenly, among guys across the social spectrum, there is a growing recognition that this business of allowing women to dictate the terms of the ongoing exchange between the sexes was a disaster," he writes. It is a revolt that Stein endorses and that two years later *Esquire* celebrated with a feature article entitled "The Second Coming of the Alpha Male." But what neither Stein nor *Esquire* will do is make excuses for the sexual cravenness that preceded this revolt. The faster the Liberated Man and the changes he acquiesced to can be relegated to the past, the better as far as they are concerned.[22]

■　■　■

In the literature of the sexual culture war, the Post-Liberated Man's troubles do not end, however, when he abandons the role of being a Liberated Man. He still faces a society in which feminism is a powerful force. It is a situation in many ways reminiscent of that which Huck Finn complained about a century ago, when at the end of his adventures he did not want to return home because Aunt Sally was there waiting to "sivilize" him. Huck could always "light out for the territory ahead of the rest." But within the sexual culture war of the 1990s, there is no such free space. What in the end defines its most imaginative literature is that it cannot conceive of a realistic context in which a crippling feminism — often a free-floating feminist anger — will not finally overwhelm any Post-Liberated Man who challenges it.

Lake Woebegon author Garrison Keillor's treatment of the Post-Liberated Man in his 1993 collection of satirical stories, *The Book of Guys*, is typical. Keillor opens his book with an introductory chapter that describes a Robert Bly–like gathering of men. Keillor writes sympathetically about the aims of the gathering. The idea of men becoming more independent and discarding their ties to the sentimentalized Liberated Man of the seventies and eighties appeals to him, and in the parts of the opening chapter where he allows his own voice to take over, Keillor makes no effort to hide his biases. "Years ago, manhood was an opportunity for achievement, and now it is a problem to be overcome," he writes in a passage that sums up his anger with feminism. "We are lovers and artists and adventurers, meant to be noble, free-ranging, and foolish, like dogs, not competing for a stamp of approval, *Friend of Womanhood*."[23]

For Keillor, it is a mistake for a man to try to be a "guy who women consider Acceptable." He can only be mediocre at it. "Men can never be feminists. Millions have tried and nobody did better than C+," he insists. It is these same feelings that make him want to see the Bly-like gathering of men he describes succeed, but the longer the gathering goes on, the more bathetic it becomes. The men can only tell stories of being wronged by women, and when it comes to breaking free, they cannot seem to get beyond adolescence. The closest they come to talking about the kind of independence Keillor thinks is important occurs when a large bearded man steps up before them and warns, "We're selling out our manhood, bit by bit, trying to buy a little peace and quiet, and you know something? It won't work. Self-betrayal never works. I say nuts to sensitivity. Go ahead and fart."[24]

After this, the men's gathering goes down hill, and a similar downhill pattern is true for the stories in *The Book of Guys*. As Keillor in a parody of Bly tries to update the heroic male myths of the past, he finds the Post-Liberated

Men who try to live these myths fail horribly when they run up against the feminist women in their lives. In "Lonesome Shorty," an independent cowboy turns into a bank robber rather than continue to live with a woman who thinks he needs to talk more and can never forgive him for not liking the local play she stars in "about good women who nurture and heal and the men who rob and control." In "Herb Johnson, the God of Canton," a football hero turns into a fat circus freak after his future wife, a football coach who is "tall, blonde, tough as nails," persuades him to play while injured and causes him to become a cripple. And in "Zeus the Lutheran," the God himself becomes impotent when the minister's wife he lusts after — a woman who dreams of divorcing her husband and taking women's studies at Bryn Mawr — proves so controlling and self-righteous that she kills his ardor.[25]

As pessimistic as Keillor about the future of the Post-Liberated Man — but without his comedic touch — is Pulitzer Prize–winning playwright David Mamet. In his *Oleanna*, which was first staged in 1992, when the controversy over Anita Hill's sexual harassment testimony against Clarence Thomas was still fresh in people's minds, Mamet offers up a drama of what happens when a very innocent Post-Liberated Man is charged with harassment by a woman who finds everything about him threatening. The man, John, is a fortyish professor. The woman, Carol, is a student of his who claims she does not understand him or his course. What happens between them reverses the assumptions that most intellectuals and liberals made about the Thomas-Hill clash. In *Oleanna* the student, with the aid of her "group" of women "who suffer what I suffer," ends up controlling the man and using her subordinate position to undo him. Over the course of three meetings they have in his office, John is transformed from a man who is supremely confident in himself and his ideas to someone who finds that Carol's charges have not only cost him his job but may land him in jail for attempted rape.[26]

In their first meeting John takes pity on Carol, who is failing his course. To get her to stop worrying about her grade, he tells her that he will give her an A if she meets with him and tries to work through her difficulties. "I'm talking to you as I'd talk to my son," he tells her. But by their second meeting John finds that the last thing he can do with Carol is treat her like a son or exercise his authority over her. She has filed a report with his tenure committee, accusing him, among other things, of being a "sexist," of telling her a sexually explicit story, and offering her an A if she will spend more time alone with him. When John tries to puzzle out how his good intentions have become so distorted, he gets a clue in Carol's reply. In language totally different from that which she used when he first saw her, she describes him as a "patriarch" in class, who feels "empowered" over people like her. The clichés of an over-formalized feminism have become Carol's way of speaking, and the second meeting between them ends as an angry Carol storms out of John's office while he tries to restrain her, hoping she will hear him out.[27]

By the third meeting their original roles have been completely reversed. Carol is now the one in power, and the language of feminist anger seems part of almost every sentence she utters. She speaks of John's use of "paternal prerogative" as "rape" and scolds him for his "sexual exploitiveness." Worried that she can prevent him from getting tenure, John asks her what he can do to change her evaluation of him. She tells him that she and her group will consider a deal if John removes a series of books, including his own, from his class reading list. Is it the group that has turned the formerly confused Carol into an angry ideologue who knows how to use sexual accusation as a weapon? Mamet never says. But since nothing in Carol's earlier appearances explains her character change, the only logical inference is that the group has caused it.[28]

John is, however, willing to fight Carol and her group. He doesn't suffer from the Liberated Man's guilt. "You think you can come in here with your political correctness and destroy my life?" he asks. Teaching isn't worth it, he tells Carol, if it means compromising his integrity in the way she and her group want him to. As it turns out, however, the deal Carol and her group offer John is not the worst of his problems. Carol and her group have told John's lawyer that they are thinking of charging him with attempted rape because he tried to restrain her from leaving his office on her second visit. This new charge is all John can take. He knocks Carol to the floor, and as the play closes, we see him standing over her in a rage. She and her group have cost him his academic career and possibly much more.[29]

When asked by an interviewer what led him to write *Oleanna*, Mamet observed, "That's like asking Capa why he took pictures of war." It is the sort of reply Michael Crichton might also have given if asked about his 1993 novel *Disclosure* and the Barry Levinson movie version of it, starring Michael Douglas and Demi Moore. In Crichton's story the Post-Liberated Man is Tom Sanders, a division manager at Digital Communications Technology in Seattle. On the day he expects to be promoted, Tom learns that the job has instead been given to his former girlfriend, Meredith Johnson. Holding his disappointment in check, he accepts her invitation to meet with him in her office at the end of the day. When Meredith attempts to renew their relationship, Tom, a married man with two children, resists. The scene ends with a furious Meredith telling him, "You walk out on me, you're dead." The next day Meredith files a sexual harassment charge against Tom, and his ordeal begins.[30]

When Tom tells his wife, a lawyer, what has happened, she is furious with him for spending time after work with Meredith and even more skeptical that he can prove what really happened. "You're a man bringing a charge of harassment against a woman. They'll laugh you out of court," she tells him. Tom, however, is a much cleverer version of the Post-Liberated Man than Mamet's professor, and he acts before he gets into deeper trouble. He hires a powerful lawyer, Louise Fernandez, who specializes in harassment cases, and with her help he is able to win in court. But the victory results primarily from a lucky break. When Meredith began propositioning Tom, he was leaving a message on a friend's answering machine. During their sexual struggle, he forgot to hang up his phone; so everything said by the two of them was recorded.[31]

Had it been a case of his word against Meredith's, it is clear that Tom would have lost his case. His lawyer tells him that, and in the book Michael Crichton makes the same point in a long paragraph in which, talking about the sexual wars of the 1990s, he describes the contemporary climate as one in which "men were assumed to be guilty of anything they were accused of." To drive home that point still deeper, Crichton makes sure that *Disclosure* does not create a happy ending in which Tom is rewarded for the unnecessary suffering he has gone through. The promotion that Tom was in line for goes to a senior woman, and his boss still thinks he was the guilty party, believing "an innocent woman took the fall for a clever, scheming man." Even more significant, Tom does not look on himself as a martyr. He feels lucky to have his old job back. His post-liberated sensibility comes without illusions. He knows that, all things being equal, his career and his marriage should have been destroyed by his encounter with Meredith Johnson.[32]

■ ■ ■

We have come, it seems, a long way from Rush Limbaugh's crude talk about feminazis. And yet when we look at what has brought about the sad endings of *Disclosure* and *Oleanna* and *The Book of Guys*, nothing could be further from the truth. For the glue of all three books is a vision of feminism that is as mean and stereotyping as anything Limbaugh serves up. Missing, to be sure, are Limbaugh's rants about feminazis and the insults that accompany the rants. But in their place is a series of portraits that are unrelenting in their depiction of woman as feminist monster. In *Disclosure* she is a power-hungry feminist monster. In *Oleanna* she is an academic feminist monster. In *The Book of Guys* she is a psychologizing feminist monster and worse. What has changed with the more nuanced writing we get in this chapter of the sexual culture war is simply that the variety of feminazi we are offered has become subtler. The only thing we don't get is the predatory sexual killer — Sharon Stone in *Basic Instinct*, Linda Fiorentino in *The Last Seduction* — that directors like Paul Verhoeven and John Dahl have made a staple of nineties film noir.

That is, however, purely a technical distinction. Although the women in *Disclosure*, *Oleanna*, and *The Book of Guys* don't kill, they might as well, given the damage they do. Crichton, Mamet, and Keillor have made it impossible for the Post-Liberated Men whose lives they touch not to hate these women as well as the feminism they embody, and as readers we are invited to follow suit.

PART THREE
Politics Without Future

7　Reporting with Attitude

████████████████████████ IT WAS THE KIND OF
story — the president of the United States receiving an
honorary degree from Oxford, where he had once been a
Rhodes Scholar — that might easily have gone unnoticed.
But it was impossible not to notice this story. *New York
Times* reporter Maureen Dowd wrote, "President Clinton
returned today for a sentimental journey to the university
where he didn't inhale, didn't get drafted, and didn't get a
degree."[1]

Dowd's one-sentence lead made indelible what in the
1990s has become the most important trend in political
reporting: the rise of a style of presidential coverage in
which the essential ingredient is a one-upmanship best described as "attitude." The attitude may be hard edge or
soft; it doesn't matter. The key is that the writer invariably
defines the president in terms of his personal foibles rather
than his policies, thus shrinking the president in stature

and putting him in the position of being the writer's inferior, a figure whom it is easy to patronize.[2]

Dowd's lead for her June 9, 1994, story on Clinton was
attitude journalism with a hard edge. In a sentence that
evoked in its parallelisms a mock Churchillian prose, she
was able to characterize the president in terms of his puta-
tive flaws: his use of marijuana, his avoidance of service in
Vietnam, his tendency to leave things incomplete. It was
not necessary for Dowd to say whether she considered
these flaws major or minor or whether she thought, for instance on Vietnam, that there might be a political explanation for Clinton's actions. At the center of the new
presidential reporting is not deep research or political
analysis so much as a combination of personal denigration
and character sketch. It is the catchy — preferably incrim-
inating — detail that matters most. In the case of Maureen
Dowd's story, she was able to take a ceremonial occasion
and turn it into ridicule by suggesting that Oxford was
simply sucking up to someone powerful and that the powerful man the university was sucking up to had in fact been
a feckless student when he was a Rhodes scholar.

The new style of presidential reporting did not arrive
overnight. It grew out of a pattern of insider reporting that
ever since Theodore White's *The Making of the President,
1960* has emphasized the behind-the-scenes political story.
Just as Joe McGinniss's 1972 *The Selling of the President*
was the natural successor to White's book, and Sidney
Blumenthal's 1980 *The Permanent Campaign* was the natural successor to McGinniss's book, so the new presidential

reporting, with its emphasis on attitude, has been the natural successor to a style of political coverage in which the insider story has become increasingly personal. By the 1990s the insider story could hardly get much more personal, but it could get meaner and more cynical.

■　　■　　■

Maureen Dowd has argued that she was practicing her version of the new presidential coverage when George Bush was still in the White House. "During the Bush years," she has insisted, "I did irreverent stories that tweaked George Bush for being out-of-touch or inarticulate." But it is with the Clinton administration that the new presidential reporting has flourished, becoming the basis of not only mainstream articles but an outpouring of books that have sought to provide a running chronicle of the Clinton years in a "gotcha atmosphere."[3]

The eagerness to get at Clinton personally was signaled during 1992, when *The New Republic* began running what it called the "Clinton Suck-Up Watch." The title of the watch, which appeared on *The New Republic*'s Notebook page, was meant to be a joke, but the impact of the watch notes, which flourished from 1992 to 1994, was anything but a joke. It didn't take much for a reporter to get into the "Clinton Suck-Up Watch." Saying that the president was better than his three predecessors in the White House could do it. So could describing him as "tireless" and "resilient" or saying he was one of the "most charming men" around and admiring the way he connected with people emotionally. What the column really worked to do was create an atmosphere in which favorable coverage of the president drew ridicule, and a mocking piece, in the tradition of the "Clinton Suck-Up Watch," got a free pass.[4]

It was not, however, until the following year that it became clear how widespread the new style in presidential coverage was becoming. The turning point came when, with the Clinton administration less than a half-year old, *Time* magazine appeared on the newsstands with a June 7 cover that proclaimed "The Incredible Shrinking President." A tiny Bill Clinton stared helplessly up from the bottom of the page, as if he were about to be crushed by the huge block letters hanging over him. The cover story, written by Michael Duffy, lived up to its title. It did not explore policy decisions, the Reagan-Bush deficit, or the president's 43 percent victory in any detail. Instead, it focused on the subjective view that the president was too small for the job. Ross Perot was quoted as saying that in any company he owned he wouldn't give Clinton a job above middle management, and, as the article made clear in its discussion of what it called Clinton's management style, *Time* agreed. The president was chided for giving too many people walk-in privileges to the Oval Office, for talking too long in meetings, for rambling in his speeches.[5]

A more personally disciplined president who was willing to adopt a more conservative course, *Time* hinted, could succeed. But the dismissive tone of the cover story and the columns accompanying it showed that the editors held out scant hope. The "stench of failure" hangs over the

White House, one column began. Another told of Clinton asking a TV reporter to help him with his makeup, as if the request were a terrible gaffe. And on it went. It was clear that Clinton was being written off by *Time* as a man who lacked the right stuff.[6]

Newsweek's cover story for the same week took almost the identical position; the difference was a matter of emphasis. Clinton, though dwarfed by the *Newsweek* headline "What's Wrong?" was at least shown looking serious as he pondered what to do about the "mess in the White House." In *Newsweek*'s story, written by Joe Klein, more attention was paid to what the president was trying to accomplish. But the patronizing tone of Klein's story, his sense that the president's personal foibles told us who he was nonetheless dominated all else. Describing the president cozying up to a television audience, Klein observed sarcastically, "He exploited the audience's empathy for the plight of a poor young president — they felt *his* pain — every last little blemish transformed into leprosy by a ravenous, irrational press." A few sentences later, Klein dropped his sarcasm for a succession of rhetorical questions. "Had we, as a nation, done it again? Had we put another turkey in the Oval Office?" And finally, as the article moved to its conclusion, Klein pictured Clinton's management problems as "chronic," a sort of incurable disease that followed him wherever he went. Like *Time*, *Newsweek* left little room for viewing the president in anything but a patronizing light.[7]

In 1993 it was not, however, only the president who

was the target of the new presidential coverage but, in a foreshadowing of things to come, also Hillary Clinton. The key article was a *New York Times Magazine* cover story by Michael Kelly entitled "Saint Hillary." The photo on the magazine's cover of Mrs. Clinton in a white suit against a white background and, inside, a drawing of her dressed as Joan of Arc, complete with sword and halo, signaled the tone of Kelly's story. "She is forty-five now, and she knows that the earnest idealisms of the 1960s may strike some people as naive or trite or grandiose. But she holds them without any apparent sense of irony or inadequacy," Kelly wrote. "She would like people to live in a way that more closely follows the Golden Rule. She would like to do good, on a grand scale, and she would like others to do good as well." For Kelly, anybody who thought that way needed to be brought down a peg, and what follows in "Saint Hillary" is a portrait in which virtually everything the president's wife does is wrong. When she acknowledges the immensity of her hopes, Kelly points up her hubris. When she tries to express her beliefs in theological terms, he criticizes her language ("a mix of Bible and Bill Moyers, New Testament and New Age"). And when she speaks concretely of her plans, he questions her authority, asking, "If it is necessary to remake society, why should Hillary Clinton get the job?"[8]

A year later, when Maureen Dowd published her account of Bill Clinton at Oxford, the stage had been set for a style of presidential reporting in which Dowd's brand of meanness — "caricature assassination," critic Katherine

Boo would call it — came as no surprise. In 1994 it was not, however, only Dowd's generation of reporters who found the new style of presidential reportage congenial. In *On the Edge*, her account of the Clinton administration's first eighteen months in office, veteran Washington reporter and former *New Yorker* writer Elizabeth Drew, turned out a book that was just as biting and personal in its portrait of the president as Dowd had been in her articles. The difference was that where Dowd was hip and acerbic, Drew was a Victorian and scold. At the start of the year, in a Sunday *Times Magazine* column, Dowd had tartly written, "Bill Clinton will never be the traditional president as father figure; he's the first president as gifted adolescent." Drew, by contrast, focused on what she called the president's "immaturity." But in terms of the new attitude reporting, it was a distinction without a difference.[9]

In his review of *On the Edge* author Nicholas Lemann put Drew in the category of nineteenth-century dispatch writers, whose technique is to recount events in a leisurely, affectless tone. For such writers, Lemann observed, the convention is that personal opinion can come only in the form of slightly ironic asides. In Drew's case there was, however, nothing slightly ironic about her asides. Deep and cutting, they revealed a president whose problems, as far as Drew was concerned, were a mirror of his personal foibles.[10]

Drew writes early on that Bill Clinton had no idea of how "unready" he was to govern, and she makes her point by arguing that he was too eager to please. She observes that even before he became president, his desire to have a diverse cabinet showed he could be influenced by pressure groups, and soon after she makes a similar criticism of Clinton's weakness with regard to his policy on gays in the military. Clinton was, she notes, too deferential to the joint chiefs when he first met with them on this subject. Could Clinton have had a diverse cabinet without taking seriously the demands of pressure groups? Would being tough with the joint chiefs have made acceptance of gays in the military easier? Drew never says. Like Maureen Dowd discussing Clinton and the draft without dealing with the Vietnam War, this is not the kind of political question Drew wants to pursue. She is content to imply that if Clinton had a different personality, he would not have had these problems. Ronald Reagan, she longingly recalls, knew how to change course and still "look like what people thought a president should look like."[11]

For Drew, explaining Clinton's problems in the White House thus becomes inseparable from offering up a denigrating portrait of him as a person. Drew can't quite convince herself that she is dealing with an adult so much as an annoying younger brother or son. She takes it as her right to be peeved with Clinton for talking too much or having a temper tantrum. She even informs us, with a certain amount of disdain, of the president's eating habits. "Clinton was a man of large appetites. He ate a lot," she writes, after she has earlier shown him eating take-out pizza against the orders of the Secret Service and conducting a meeting in which Pepperidge Farm cookies are in constant circulation.[12]

At one point Drew even offers an explanation for why the president seems immature. Perhaps it was "because he was his proud mother's perfect son, or because for all the rough-and-tumble of politics he hadn't lived in the real world very much and had so many of his needs, psychic or material, catered to," she speculates. But for Drew, explanations or hard proofs for her ideas don't in the long run matter or change the fact that this is a president she can't help patronizing. "Other Presidents had tempers. Eisenhower's was famously bad," Drew concedes. "The real significance of Clinton's temper was what it said about his deeper nature. There was a self-indulgence in Clinton's tantrums, an immaturity, a part of him that never grew up," she writes. "There seemed to be something unfinished about him. Compared to many men his age, or even younger, he didn't seem quite grown up."[13]

Over the course of *On the Edge* the result is that even though Drew admits that Clinton achieved a lot in his first year in office, she still views him as someone who can't do things right. His "demystification of the presidency" is a flaw in her eyes. So is his "penchant for being agreeable" and so is his sixties-style willingness to hear people out. When the president as a joke puts on a reporter's Mickey Mouse tie or answers a question about the kind of undershorts he wears, it only confirms for Drew her worst doubts. In her epilogue, when Drew quotes Bill Clinton telling his aide Leon Panetta, who is urging him to remain more distant from the public, "I've got to be more like John Wayne," we get the perfect conclusion to *On the Edge*. Here stands the quintessential tall, silent movie hero, and there is Clinton, like a child, wishing for what Drew has taken great pains to show he can never be.[14]

■   ■   ■

Among journalism watchers, the changes in political reporting in general and presidential reporting in particular that have been occurring in the nineties have not gone unnoticed. Early in the decade the prime criticism of political reporting was that its focus on media issues and campaign tactics prevented serious consideration of politics. In his 1990 essay, "Blips, Bites, and Savvy Talk," Todd Gitlin took this line of attack, pointing up how campaign journalism had become obsessed with the horse-race aspect of elections and from there moved on to a metacoverage of elections that avoided political substance for a backstage look at how modern political campaigns used the media. Two years later in *Dirty Politics* Kathleen Hall Jamieson picked up where Gitlin left off, contending that the media, by virtue of its belief that strategy now told what was important about a political campaign, not only missed out on substantive questions but in effect invited the voters to see themselves as spectators watching the performance of people who were bent on manipulating them. The one exception to this line of criticism was a prescient essay in 1992 by Katherine Boo in the *Washington Monthly* that focused on how the new "warts-and-all journalism" of writers like Maureen Dowd was creating a style of political reporting in which sneering was an art form and stories were as "attitudinous as Pucci prints."[15]

But by 1994 essays like Boo's were no longer the exception. A very different kind of concern with political coverage had come into play, focusing on how the end of objectivity and an increase in "attitude" were making meanness and denigration central to mainstream political writing. The new focus was expressed at the start of the year by *New York Times* columnist Michiko Kakutani in an essay entitled "Opinion vs. Reality in an Age of Pundits." Belief in objectivity, Kakutani argued, was becoming obsolete. "Throughout our culture," she wrote, "the old notions of 'truth' and 'knowledge' are in danger of being replaced by the new ones of 'opinion,' 'perception,' and 'credibility.'" Kakutani felt that this development applied to everything from talk radio to fiction, but her point had special relevance for political reporting and the growing emphasis on attitude, both hidden and overt. There was, as Kakutani's essay noted, increasingly little reason for writers to try to rein in their own biases and, more important, their anger.[16]

Six months later in another *New York Times* essay, "When Fact Is Treated as Fiction," literary critic James Atlas, focusing on Bob Woodward's *The Agenda*, picked up where Kakutani left off, noting how in books like Woodward's it had become "harder to distinguish fact from gossip" or to know what to trust. The real follow-up to Kakutani's essay came later in 1994, however, in an essay by Jacob Weisberg praising Bill Clinton. For Weisberg, the underestimation of Clinton was inseparable from the media's treatment of him. But for Weisberg, the reason for that treatment was only secondarily explained by the personal distrust of Clinton so many reporters had. The most significant change, as far as Weisberg was concerned, came from the nature of "the new political journalism."

In an effort to add to the information that could instantly be gotten from CNN and the wire services, a growing number of political journalists, Weisberg contended, had come to feel they had to put "an edge of judgment" on whatever they reported. The catch was that this edge no longer came primarily from investigation but from digging dirt and exploring personalities. It was based on "an evolution from reporting to analysis to psychoanalysis," and what it meant was that the edge the new political reporting supplied finally had more in common with the opening monologues of late-night talk shows than with traditional reportage. "*The Washington Post* toppled Nixon with its reporting. It's bringing Clinton down with attitude," Weisberg argued. Even more significant, Weisberg concluded, by some sort of Gresham's law of the media, the new attitude reporting was crowding out the work of examining political programs and policies.[17]

By 1996 this view was far more widespread among journalism watchers. In *The New Yorker* it was the basis of media critic James Wolcott's analysis of Maureen Dowd's "persistent razzing" of the president for everything from being too empathetic to going on food binges. And in

Esquire it was the source of civil rights historian Taylor Branch's assertion that the contempt he found in the political profiles of Bill Clinton put the president on a different planet from the man Branch saw in the White House and had known since they worked in Texas for George McGovern.[18]

At the same time, two very different books, one on the media and one on politics, put the new political reporting and presidential coverage in an even larger perspective by way of accounting for the kinds of meanness and spite that had come to dominate it. In *Breaking the News: How the Media Undermine American Democracy*, *U.S. News* editor James Fallows argued that we are now caught up in "an arms race of 'attitude,' in which reporters don't explicitly argue or analyze what they like in a political program but instead sound sneering and supercilious." The reaction by politicians and their handlers, Fallows went on to say, has been to become more manipulative in trying to get their message past the press — with the result that the press has fought back by raising the political arms race in attitude to still higher levels. In *They Only Look Dead: Why Progressives Will Dominate the Next Political Era*, veteran *Washington Post* reporter E. J. Dionne made a similar argument. Picking up where Michiko Kakutani left off, Dionne argued that in abandoning standards of objectivity and fairness for the sake of mean-spirited combat, what we have ended up with is livelier writing that doesn't actually enliven debate. Epithets and cleverness, Dionne concluded, have replaced thoughtfulness and made it easier than ever for voters to disparage politics and politicians while losing track of the distinctions between fact and opinion, information and mere assertion.[19]

■ ■ ■

Since Michiko Kakutani's "Opinion vs. Reality in an Age of Pundits" was first published, there has been significant presidential coverage that has escaped the attitude trap. Connie Bruck's 1994 *New Yorker* profile, "Hillary the Pol," which focused on the Clinton administration as well as on the president's wife, stayed remarkably free from attitude, and since then so have two highly critical Clinton books. In *Washington Post* reporter David Maraniss's *First in His Class* we get a meticulously researched book that is very tough on Clinton, especially with regard to the draft, but that takes him seriously and works hard to explain the likes and dislikes Maraniss felt for the pre-presidential Clinton. The same is true of investigative reporter James Stewart's *Blood Sport*, which examines Whitewater and uncovers no legal wrongdoing by the president but still finds the Clintons lacking in candor about their finances and past behavior.[20]

Nonetheless, over the last two years the kind of presidential coverage epitomized by Maureen Dowd and by *Time*'s shrinking-president issue has increased, not decreased, in intensity. Nothing makes this escalation of attitude clearer than the example of *Primary Colors*, Joe Klein's roman à clef about Bill Clinton and his 1992 presidential campaign. Originally published anonymously,

Primary Colors quickly became the book for people who didn't read anything else about Clinton, selling over a million copies in its first year and getting bought by Hollywood for a Mike Nichols movie. In its story of an ambitious southern politician as seen through the eyes of his disillusioned aide, *Primary Colors* invites comparison with Robert Penn Warren's portrait of Huey Long in *All the King's Men*. The comparison is, however, one that doesn't go far. In *All the King's Men* Warren grappled with the larger issues of populism and the Depression and how a modern democracy works. What gives *Primary Colors* its reason for being is its presentation of a philandering Bill Clinton look-alike candidate, whose sexual wanderings and double dealings are portrayed as the center of his life.[21]

In Warren's fictionalized version of Huey Long, it was possible to ask what faults were tolerable in a politician who reached people and who could do something to lessen their suffering. But in *Primary Colors* there is no room for ambiguity about presidential candidate Jack Stanton. His character is nailed shut on the novel's first page with his aide Henry Burton's description of him shaking hands. "He is a genius with it," Henry observes. "He is interested in you. He is honored to meet you. . . . If he doesn't know you all that well and you've just told him something 'important,' something earnest or emotional, he will lock in and honor you with a two-hander, his left hand overwhelming your wrist and forearm. He'll flash that famous misty look of his. And he will mean it." Henry stays with Jack Stanton until he learns that the candidate has slept with the teenage daughter of a local supporter, but over the course of the book, the only real question is when Henry will realize what he has gotten himself into. As Susan, Jack Stanton's wife, tells him on their first meeting, "Jack Stanton could be a great man if he weren't such a faithless, thoughtless, disorganized, undisciplined shit."[22]

Klein's style in *Primary Colors* and in a series of *Newsweek* essays on Clinton has increasingly become the norm in presidential coverage. Instead of becoming more subtle — of making attitude a matter of implication — presidential coverage has gone in the opposite direction, more than fulfilling *Arkansas Democrat-Gazette* columnist Gene Lyons's remark that in recent years "Bill and Hillary Rodham Clinton have been treated with the kind of gleeful malice formerly reserved for Donald Trump and Marla Maples, Bruce Willis and Demi Moore."[23]

In the most recent coverage of Clinton, it is often hard to see him as a president who doesn't deserve our unlimited contempt for the way he carries himself through life. In Richard Reeves's *Running in Place: How Bill Clinton Disappointed America* the president is "a surfer politician, waiting on the board, looking back toward the horizon, confident he will see the first hint of the next big wave, then ride high wherever it takes him." In Camille Paglia's *New Republic* profile of Hillary Clinton, the president is the New Man turned skirt chaser, someone whose "aw-shucks rap is one of the most effective womanizing styles of all time." And even in the *New York Times Magazine* the president can't seem to be much more than the laundry list of foibles

Susan Stanton checks off when she sums up her husband's character for Henry Burton.[24]

In Todd Purdum's 1996 *Times Magazine* cover story, "Facets of Clinton," we get at the start a long recitation of Bill Clinton's successes and failures. But the Clinton who dominates Purdum's piece is finally not a figure to be analyzed in political terms so much as a character to be watched as he "rolls around the universe like a pinball in a machine." He is a man who eats too much, who screws too much (or thinks about screwing too much), and who is incapable of sincerity. Clinton has, Purdum insists, already used up eight and a half of a politician's nine allotted lives and is working away at the last half life. Clinton, according to Purdum, is capable of dropping a friend for political reasons, but at the same time he never stops trying to win over strangers. What becomes him most are roles. At the start of his presidency, he was in Purdum's eyes a man-child running the West Wing of the White House like a pizza party. Later he was a tenderfoot lurching through the issue of homosexuals in the army. And by 1995 he was Braveheart, reassuring the nation after the Oklahoma City bombing tragedy. Sex — or as Purdum calls it, "Clinton's reputation for libidinal overdrive" — is never far away. "If Clinton invariably makes men comfortable with a 'Nice tie,' when he shakes their hands," Purdum writes, "he is just as quick to drop his eyes to a woman's décolletage and murmur, "Nice pin!" By the end of his profile, Purdum has not only revisited every known Clinton foible, he has declared the passage in *Primary Colors* about Jack Stanton seducing supporters with the fraudulent sincerity of his handshake possibly "the best word-picture of the Clinton treatment ever put on paper."[25]

In Purdum's profile the reference to Joe Klein's novel comes by way of analogy. It allows Purdum to point up the self-deception and callowness he sees in Clinton. But in terms of where the new presidential coverage of the nineties is taking us, the analogy is revealing in another way as well. It captures how the new style of presidential coverage, in blurring the distinction between what is factually true and what is simply asserted, has created an atmosphere in which readers care less about the accuracy of a presidential story than about the impression it allows them to take away. In 1994, when the conservative journalist David Brock published an article in *The American Spectator*, "Living with the Clintons," that took at face value the stories of two Arkansas troopers about the Clintons' sex lives, the article was dismissed by most of the media not only because it couldn't be authenticated but because the descriptions of Bill and Hillary Clinton defied credulity. From the account of Bill Clinton's eating habits ("He would pick up a baked potato with his hands and eat it in two bites.") to the picture of Vincent Foster, Hillary Clinton's law partner, publicly squeezing her rear and running his hand over her breast, Brock's vignettes seemed to be based on nothing but malice. By the time he got around to stories of Bill Clinton receiving oral sex while sitting in a parked car outside the governor's compound or seducing women during his morning jogs, it was hard to take anything he reported seriously.[26]

These days, accounts like Brock's are not readily dismissed, however. A very real byproduct of attitude journalism has been a lowering of skepticism toward any book about Clinton that manages to stoke the right resentment. A perfect example is Richard Morris's bestseller *Partners in Power: The Clintons and Their America*. Morris's take on the Clintons is never in doubt. Attitude isn't subtle here. Clinton is a man who weeps on cue, who is craven and vacillating, whose frequent church-going is a pretense, and who, along with his wife, is "emblematic of the larger bipartisan system at its end-of-the-century dead end." But what gives Morris's book its bite is his willingness to flesh out his feelings about Clinton on the basis of evidence that either takes the research of a figure like David Brock at face value or else relies on "confidential sources" we are assured can be trusted. By the end of *Partners in Power* we don't just get Clinton as the father of a black child, the seducer of "literally hundreds of women," and a regular coke user. He is also someone who was a knowing supporter of the Nicaraguan contras and condoned a drug smuggling and arms shipment operation, overseen by the CIA, that was conducted out of the airport at Mena, Arkansas.[27]

Even more fantastical is a book that dominated the news in the days following its publication and also quickly made it onto the bestseller list. In former FBI agent Gary Aldrich's *Unlimited Access: An FBI Agent Inside the White House* the story is the ongoing crimes and misdemeanors of the president. Like Morris, Aldrich makes no secret of his contempt for the Clintons and their values. Style matters to him, and while he doesn't have Maureen Dowd's eye for reporting it, he does have her habit of using it to define presidential character. For Aldrich the shabby values of the Clinton administration are visible everywhere he turns. The men around Clinton wear scuffed shoes. The women put on dresses that make the White House look like Hooters, and everyone on staff seems to treat the White House as if it were a college dorm. Worst of all for Aldrich are the morals of the Clintonites. "I was disappointed when I discovered that the vice president's staff was not much different than the Clinton staff," Aldrich writes. "They too had serious character flaws which were reflective of their counter-culture roots, including a casual attitude about the use of drugs." The result for Aldrich is that the Clintons themselves can do no right. Even their Christmas tree ornaments are tacky compared to those of the Bushes. Aldrich's biggest shocker for his readers is, however, the conduct of the president himself. What Todd Purdum called "libidinal overdrive," what other journalists in their attitude pieces saw as an incapacity for honesty, Aldrich tells us is literally true.[28]

"It appears that the president is a frequent late-night visitor to the Marriott Hotel in downtown Washington, which has an underground parking garage with an elevator that allows guests to go to their rooms without passing through the lobby," Aldrich reports. "The president does not have a room in his name, and the guest who rents the room is known only to the management, though some information indicates this individual is female and may be a celebrity." And on it goes, getting still worse. "The president's driver is believed to be Bruce Lindsey, a high-level White House staffer and longtime friend of the president," Aldrich writes. "The car is parked near the elevator. The driver waits in the car until the president returns, often hours later. The car usually arrives after midnight and sometimes leaves early in the morning, sometimes as late as 4:00 A.M." It is a defining moment for *Unlimited Access*, as well as for attitude journalism and its spinoffs. Presidential coverage doesn't get any juicier than this.[29]

■ ■ ■

Reviewing *Unlimited Access* in the *New York Times*, Maureen Dowd focused on the provincialism of Aldrich's personal criticisms of the Clintons and their aides. "Has agent Aldrich never been to Manhattan?" she asked after a passage in which Aldrich complained about a Clinton staffer wearing black pants, a black T-shirt, and black lipstick. On the West Coast, critic Suzanne Garment, writing in the *Los Angeles Times*, took the same line, tartly observing of Aldrich's criticism of style in the White House that earrings and ponytails on men are not the end of civilization. What neither Dowd nor Garment would do, however, was wrestle with what the presence of so much unverified gossip in *Unlimited Access* did to Aldrich's credibility as a whole. In giving him a free pass on this, they were not, however, alone. Even before *Unlimited Access* was published, the *Wall Street Journal* gave Aldrich its stamp of approval, printing excerpts from the book and endorsing his criticism of White House security. And in the week Aldrich's book came out, it was a major story in newspapers across the country and on network television. By Sunday he was a featured guest on ABC's *This Week with David Brinkley*. Things didn't change until David Brock, Aldrich's "secret" source for the tales of Clinton's midnight trysts, publicly acknowledged that he had no direct knowledge of them, and Aldrich responded that trysts were simply a "possibility" that could not be discounted. Only then did Aldrich fall into the category of discredited writer and programs like CNN's *Larry King Live* and NBC's *Dateline* cancel their scheduled interviews with him.[30]

It is the seriousness with which Aldrich was initially taken, rather than his fall from grace, that tells us the most about the new presidential journalism of the nineties, however. It was against all odds that Aldrich was caught in the way he was. Rarely is one person able to undermine a book's credibility overnight and force its author to admit that his most sensational revelation — recounted in detail — is simply a possibility. On the other hand, it was easy for Aldrich initially to gain access to the most important newspapers and television shows in the country. In the atmosphere created by attitude journalism, there is not only a desire for reporting that gives us a chance to sneer at the president, there is a desperation for anything — alleged incidents, unconfirmed stories, speculation — that will give shape to our sneering.[31]

In *Breaking the News* James Fallows argues that end of the Cold War has made it safer to sneer at and patronize the president. He is no longer the man we count on to protect us from nuclear war. It is an argument that makes sense, and when we add to it the reduced role, typified by the devolution of welfare programs to the states, that the federal government has come to play in domestic policy, we have still another reason why it is easier these days to look down on the president. None of this would, however, be happening if it were not for a journalism that sees politics as a game and catching the president out — viewing him with attitude — as a sign that a reporter is at the top of his or her form.[32]

As the 1996 election showed, there is simply no penalty for a reporter showing too much attitude. The *Washington Post* did not finally run, as rumor had it would, a September story about an affair Bob Dole had in the 1960s while he was still married to his first wife, but the *Post*'s restraint was the exception, not the rule, in 1996. When the story of Clinton aide Dick Morris's affair with a prostitute broke, it got far more attention on television and in the mainstream press than Morris's role in formulating Clinton's reelection strategy ever did, and throughout the campaign nothing was off limits. In the fall of 1996 Clinton's health became an issue not because, in contrast to the much older Bob Dole, he seemed unhealthy but because rumors circulated, as reporter Chris Matthews told a national audience on *Good Morning America*, that Clinton had a sexually transmitted disease. Reporters were never able to confirm that Clinton had such a disease, but as White House transcripts show, they were able to get away with directly asking his press secretary if he did. "Good God, do you really want to ask that question?" Clinton press secretary Michael McCurry asked back. But the calmness of his rejoinder was what was revealing. To the administration the question was embarrassing, but above all, it was a sign of the new presidential journalism. It didn't pay, as *New Yorker* writer Ken Auletta pointed out in a postelection essay "Inside Story: Why Did Both Candidates Despise the Press?" for a press secretary to get angry with such a question unless he wanted to provoke a great many more just like it. "Cynicism," as CNN White House correspondent Claire Shipman told Auletta, "has been adopted as a way to be seen as fair, as a way to view both sides."[33]

Where, in terms of the near future, we are headed with attitude journalism may be seen in the reaction of most reporters to Joe Klein's revelation that he was, after all, the author of *Primary Colors*. There had been speculation for some time that Klein was the book's anonymous author, but Klein vehemently denied it, even calling *New York* magazine, where he once worked, to protest an article by Vassar professor Donald Foster that used computer textual analysis to argue that Klein was the author of *Primary Colors*. When Klein confessed that he had been lying all along after a handwriting expert hired by the *Washington Post* to examine a manuscript of *Primary Colors* reached the same conclusion as Foster, it was thus a big news story, one large enough to force Klein to hold a press conference of his own in order to explain his actions.[34]

But among Klein's colleagues, the reaction to his revelations was, with few exceptions, mild. Criticism tended to be limited either to saying he should have come clean earlier, rather than continue to lie, or that *Newsweek*, the magazine for which he wrote at the time, should not have printed a "Periscope" column suggesting another writer was the author of *Primary Colors*. Typical was the reaction of *New Republic* literary editor Leon Wieseltier, who in his magazine's "Washington Diarist" column observed of Klein, "I know that he lied. I forgive him and am delighted for him. I would have lied, too. It was not a lie that in any way did me damage." For most of his fellow reporters, it was enough for Joe Klein to assure them, "Joe Klein has never lied in a column and never will." They never thought to ask whether, after writing a highly successful novel attributing an enormously deceptive sexual and personal life to the president, Klein might not have a stake in supporting such a view of the president in his columns. In the age of attitude journalism, it was as if such a question only mattered to the naive reader, unaware of the new rules in presidential reporting.[35]

8 The Contract of 1996

IN THE SPRING OF
1996, Bill Clinton and Bob Dole suddenly found themselves caught up in the kind of personal exchange the modern presidential campaign fosters. Who, Bob Dole asked
the public, would you rather have for your children's
baby sitter, me or Bill Clinton? Clinton's reply came soon
afterward at a White House correspondents' dinner. He
would, he joked, be a much better baby sitter than Bob
Dole. He would let the kids play Nintendo in the Situation
Room. To drive home his point that kids would have
more fun with him, he asked the correspondents, who
they would rather have select their pizza toppings, him or
Bob Dole.[1]

The Clinton-Dole baby-sitter exchange drew plenty
of laughs, but behind its silliness was a meanness that went
to the heart of the 1996 presidential campaign. In their
baby-sitter exchange Clinton and Dole finally weren't
joking. They were sending coded messages to the voters,

calculated to put each other in the worst possible light. Do you really want someone with Bill Clinton's history and unreliability watching over your kids? Dole was asking. Do you really want someone as old and rigid as Bob Dole making the decisions that could affect your day-to-day life? Clinton was asking back.

The *Washington Post* took the baby-sitter question seriously enough to poll people on it (Clinton won by a margin of 56 to 20 percent), and by fall the television ads of the two candidates openly dealt with what their baby-sitter jibes had implied. The Dole ads portrayed Clinton as irresponsible and showed clips from his 1992 MTV appearance in which he had laughed about trying to smoke marijuana. The Clinton television ads, in turn, emphasized Dole's age, harking back to his early opposition to Medicare in the 1960s. The politics behind the baby-sitter jokes and the ads was in both cases a direct borrowing from the 1980s. For Dole, the aim was to repeat the 1988 campaign that George Bush had successfully waged against Michael Dukakis by portraying him as a liberal who was out of touch with mainstream values. For Clinton, the aim was to repeat Ronald Reagan's 1984 reelection campaign against Walter Mondale, in which he portrayed Mondale as a politician from another era while positioning himself as the defender of such popular government programs as Medicare and Social Security.[2]

The strategy was one that the media caught on to early in the game and that the candidates' advisers made no attempt to hide. "We haven't found Willie Horton, but we have found William Clinton," observed Scott Reed, Dole's campaign manager. Ann Lewis, Clinton's deputy campaign manager, was even blunter. "They want to re-play 1988 over and over, but we're not going to play," she declared. The "model" for how to reelect a president, she went on to say, was Ronald Reagan in 1984. The result was not, however, just a campaign based on the tactics of the 1980s. It was also a campaign fought on Republican turf, with both candidates shaping their rhetoric and their pro-grams to appeal to the same middle-class electorate.[3]

Given the expected low turnout among poor and mi-nority voters, this was a shrewd political turn for both sides to take. In Dole's case, however, there was little room left for maneuver. At the 1984 Republican National Conven-tion the band had played "Happy Days Are Here Again," and Ronald Reagan had quoted Roosevelt, Truman, and Kennedy to drive home his centrist appeal. But by 1996 it was difficult for Dole to move to his left without losing voters from the hard-core right, particularly the Christian Coalition, which was crucial to his base of support. Clin-ton, on the other hand, with the traditional Democratic constituency locked in, had the freedom and the need to zigzag. By the fall of 1996, his success in moving to his right had been noted by his opponents. Republicans — from Senator Jesse Helms in North Carolina to Represen-tative Phil English in Pennsylvania — saw the Clinton strategy as a winning one; to defeat their "liberal" Demo-cratic opponents they pointed out the similarities between their positions and those of the president. But success in moving to the right not only brought Clinton more votes in 1996 than in 1992, it also created a new continuum in American politics by offering middle-class voters a set of compromises they could live with. They could reject a Republican "extremism" that had frightened them ever since Newt Gingrich had been elevated to speaker of the House, but they could do so while believing they would get a leaner and meaner federal government in which the old welfare state had no place and the highest priority was deficit reduction.[4]

                 ■ ■ ■

To see how the 1996 presidential election came to uphold Bill Clinton's version of leaner and meaner government, we have to look back to the fall of 1994, when the Republicans handed Democrats their worst midterm defeat in forty years, gaining nine Senate and fifty-three House seats. For Clinton and the neoliberal wing of the Democratic party that he represented, the lesson of 1994 was that the egalitarian wing of the party, rooted in the policies of Franklin Roosevelt, was finished. In an interview he gave on the day after the election, Al From, the executive director of the Democratic Leadership Council, delivered the eulogy for the Democratic party of old. "The New Deal is over. It was a grand and glorious era for Democrats, but it is over. The nails are in the coffin of liberalism, and it is dead and buried," From observed. "The truth of the Democratic party is that there is no party. There is no base. We have lost the middle class, and instead we have minority voters, a few liberals, and union members. That's it. That's all we have left."[5]

It was not, however, only the liberal Democrats who appeared finished at the end of 1994: so did the Clinton administration. A CBS News poll showed that 78 percent of the electorate now expected Congress to have more influence over government than the president. As for Clinton, he was widely viewed as damaged beyond repair, a man who had failed in his most important undertaking — health care — and could be expected only to serve out the rest of his term on the defensive. "He has seemed lost and pathetic since the election," *Newsweek* columnist Joe Klein observed. "He has not yet figured out how to communicate with the American public in this era. It may well be that his presidency is beyond the point of no return." Liberal columnist Jack Newfield was even more outspoken. "Rank and file Democrats must help dump Clinton in order to open up more electable options for the party," he wrote in an open letter that appeared on the front page of the *New York Post.* And in a *New Yorker* interview Democratic party political consultant Ted Van Dyck sardonically asked, "Is there any Democratic senator or any Democratic congressman or any Democratic governor who wants to run with Bill Clinton at the top of the ticket in 1996? Not on your life. It's over. The President is done. He's finished."[6]

With his December 1994 approval ratings at 38 percent, the president did not have to be convinced that his situation was desperate and that if he hoped to win back the voters he had lost, he needed to move to his right and capture for himself and his administration the themes the Republicans had made central in their Contract with America. In his January 1995 State of the Union Address, the president signaled that he was willing to change, acknowledging that "last year, as the evidence indicates, we bit off more than we could chew." By the spring he had begun the process of preempting the Contract with America, coopting for himself the Republicans' commitment to balancing the budget, cutting government, and ending welfare as a federal entitlement.[7]

The new strategy, given the name "triangulation" by its chief architect, Dick Morris, who sought to place the president in a "dynamic center" that would be beyond the claims of both left and right, was at the start largely rhetorical. With Republicans firmly in control of the House and Senate, there was no way the president could redefine himself through his own legislation. The limits on the president's ability to redefine himself did not, however, deter his enthusiasm for doing so, and by midsummer, stage one of his transformation was complete. He was now the champion of a government that promised, in exchange for doing less for the poor and for minorities, to leave the middle class better off.[8]

After his 1995 State of the Union Address, the president gave the first big indication of the direction in which he intended to move in March, in a speech to the National League of Cities. Sounding like a Democratic Newt Gingrich, the president declared it was the duty of government to promote opportunity, demand responsibility, and favor mainstream values. Without ever using the word "triangulation," Clinton made it clear that he would achieve these results through triangulation. "I think we have to chart a course between and beyond the old way of big government and the new rage of no government," he declared.[9]

Three weeks later, at an April 7 speech in Dallas before the American Society of Newspaper Editors, the president spelled out in detail the political route he would take. Conceding that the Republicans had changed the political direction of the country with their November victory, the president announced that he was prepared to "keep alive the momentum and the spirit of the change." Rather than distinguishing his New Covenant from the Contract with America, the president went out of his way to emphasize their similarities. Both sides wanted, he pointed out, an end to welfare as we knew it, deficit reduction, and fewer government regulations. The real issue, the president insisted, was how best to achieve those results. "The old labels of liberal and conservative, spender and cutter, even Democrat and Republican, are not what matter most anymore," he insisted. "What matters most is finding practical, pragmatic solutions based on what we know works in our lives and our shared experiences."[10]

Only political purists, the president argued, worried that he was being inconsistent, and to make the point that he was not violating his Democratic heritage, five days later, on April 12, he used the fiftieth anniversary of

Franklin Roosevelt's death to insist that if he were alive today, FDR would have changed as well. "He wouldn't be here defending everything he did fifty years ago, he wouldn't be denying the existence of the information age," the president told his audience in Warm Springs, Georgia. To liberals within his own party, the president's move to the right was hard to take, for it was their ideas and loyalties that inevitably suffered. But within the country as a whole, the change was widely accepted, and when in the wake of the Oklahoma City Federal Building bombing, the president became the nation's chief comforter, much as Ronald Reagan had a decade earlier after the *Challenger* explosion, his standing was further enhanced.[11]

By June only one major political issue, balancing the budget, still left the president vulnerable to Republican criticism, and in a nationally televised address on June 13, he ended that difference as well, promising a balanced budget that over the next ten years would cut discretionary spending by 20 percent in every area but education. The popularity of Clinton's move to the right and his growing stature as a chief executive who seemed reassuring was reflected in the polls. On January 6 a *Washington Post*/ABC News poll showed the president losing the 1996 election by 48 to 33 percent against an unnamed Republican and trailing Bob Dole by 17 points in approval ratings. By May 1995, however, the president's approval rating had climbed to a respectable 51 percent. Two months later a July 23 CNN/*USA Today*/Gallup survey showed the president leading Bob Dole in the race for the White House by a 50 to 44 percent margin. For someone who at the end of 1994 had been described by the *New York Times* as a "deflated" president who had had the wind taken out of his sails, it was a remarkable comeback. While gaining 23 points on his chief political rival, he had publicly settled the question of whether he believed government should be reduced in size and made less responsive to the needs of the poor. It was now clear to the electorate, as Democratic pollsters Mark Penn and Douglas Schoen later put it, that the president "rejected the New Deal liberal view that government can solve almost every problem."[12]

■   ■   ■

The president was, however, far from out of the woods. A second crucial question remained for the election of 1996. Why should voters trust Bill Clinton to implement what was essentially a Republican program for making government leaner and meaner? As former Bush campaign manager Mary Matalin put it in a *Washington Post* interview, "Now he wants to be a Republican again. I guess you could say it's good politics, but why reelect him? Why not the real thing?"[13]

It was a reasonable question, and for the rest of 1995, the president's political efforts were devoted to answering the "me too" charge. In his breakthrough speech on April 7, the president had laid out the role he would play in the upcoming budget battle. "In the first one hundred days, it fell to the House of Representatives to propose. In the next one hundred days and beyond, the president has to lead the quiet, reasoned forces of both parties in both houses to sift through the rhetoric and decide what is really best for America," he had declared then. But it was not until August 1995, after he had established his commitment to a leaner and meaner government, that the president was in a position to point out how his cuts would differ from those of the Republicans.

His counterattack began in early August with two thirty-second television ads. The first, called "Protect," opened with a shot of a hospital heart monitor recording a steady heartbeat, followed by a voice-over in which an announcer declared, "Medicare. Lifeline for the elderly. There is a way to protect Medicare benefits and balance the budget." The Clinton budget plan, the ad declared, could do both. The Republicans, with their proposed two-hundred-seventy billion dollars in Medicare cuts, could not. A day later, on August 11, a second thirty-second ad, this one called "Moral," pursued the same theme, only in much more Reaganesque fashion. This time the president's Medicare stance was interwoven with pictures of children, the flag, and an elderly farmer, before the voice-over got around to saying, "We created Medicare not because it was cheap or easy. But because it was the right thing to do."[14]

The ads, produced by Dick Morris and long-time Democratic media consultant Bob Squier, were slickly done. But they depended for their effect on the Republicans playing the meanness game by showing they could be tougher with the budget than the Democrats. Had the

Republicans been willing to lessen their cuts in Medicare and make budget reductions elsewhere, they might have coopted Clinton, just as Clinton was coopting them. But rather than contest the president for the political center, the Republicans, buoyed by their new majorities in the House and Senate, took a hard line on Medicare and never answered the August ads. Then in the fall they handed Clinton the wedge he needed to minimize the fact that with his ten-year balanced-budget proposal, Medicare would also become more expensive for the elderly. On October 24 Bob Dole, meeting with a conservative group, bragged that he was one of only a dozen House members who had voted against Medicare in 1965, and on the same day Newt Gingrich, speaking about the Health Care Administration, the agency that handles Medicare payments, told a group of supporters that he believed the agency was going to "wither on the vine" as people left Medicare voluntarily. Six days later, on October 30, a third Dick Morris–Bob Squier Medicare ad, this one called "Wither," drew the line between the Clinton budget and the Republican budget even more sharply than the August ad had done. Using the Dole and Gingrich quotes from October 24, the ad declared, "Finally, we learn the truth about how the Republicans want to eliminate Medicare. The Republicans in Congress never believed in Medicare. And now they want it to wither on the vine."[15]

Dole and Gingrich both argued that they had been quoted out of context, but no amount of explaining could undo the fears their remarks had aroused. An October *New*

York Times/CBS News poll showed that the public, especially the elderly, disapproved of the Republican plan for balancing the budget and cutting welfare by a ratio of more than two to one. By November 13, when the budget impasse between Congress and the administration caused a partial shutdown of the government for six days, the president was put in a commanding position. Two days into the budget battle, a CNN/*USA Today* poll showed that 49 percent of the public blamed the Republicans for the shutdown, while just 26 percent blamed the president. Even more significant, 49 percent of the public said they trusted the Democrats to cut the budget while maintaining necessary programs, but only 36 percent said they believed the Republicans would do the same. The second stage of the president's 1996 campaign was now paying dividends. He had not only convinced voters that he accepted the Republicans' overall position on reducing government; he had convinced them that his plans for achieving a leaner and meaner government were superior to the Republicans'. As Bill Kristol, the conservative editor of the *Weekly Standard*, put it, "Clinton basically has told the voters, 'I've got it. No more grand health care plans. Now I'm the check on the Republican Congress, where I basically accommodate the direction they want to go, but I'm going to slow it down.'" What exasperated liberals within the Democratic party — the president's willingness to back away from the party's most egalitarian programs — was a plus at the national level, and before the November government shutdown was over, the president had strengthened his hand still further by agreeing to the Republicans' call for a seven-year timetable for balancing the budget.[16]

To voters the president, in contrast to Newt Gingrich and the Republican Congress, seemed to be doing his best to avoid a fight, and when on December 6, using the pen Lyndon Johnson had used in 1965 to sign Medicare and Medicaid into law, he vetoed the Republican budget, he was able to score a huge media victory, despite the fact that under his plan Medicare payments would rise from $46 a month to $77 in seven years, while under the Republicans they would rise to $85, a difference of just $8. A second shutdown of the government, this one over the Christmas holidays and extending into 1996, left Clinton in a still better position. By mid-December 61 percent of Americans said the president was really trying to find a solution to the budget crisis, while only 43 percent said the Republicans were trying as hard. As far as voters were concerned, the president was showing that he had their interests at heart. In a *New York Times*/CBS News poll, 54 percent of the respondents said the president wanted to do what was best for them and their families; only 36 percent gave the same credit to the Republicans. In terms of the upcoming presidential election, the gap was just as wide. Fifty-two percent of registered voters now said that in a general election they would vote for Bill Clinton, while 40 percent said they would cast their votes for Bob Dole. A year after the Republicans had ridden to victory on the Contract with America, Bill Clinton had not only taken their agenda and made it his own, he had convinced a majority of voters that he was the better person to see it through.[17]

■ ■ ■

Where would the president go from here? What would Dole do to stop him? As 1996 began, the presidential campaign, despite the ongoing Republican primaries, had boiled down to these two questions. The initial answer to them came in January with the president's State of the Union Address and Bob Dole's response for the Republican party.

The president's answer was that he would turn the third and final phase of his campaign into a referendum on the decision he had taken in 1995 to make government leaner and meaner. He would not, however, simply repeat the promises he had given in 1995 to reduce government and balance the budget. Over the next ten months, he would also move to preempt for himself and his party the cultural issues that lay behind so much of the economizing called for by the Contract with America.[18]

In his 1996 State of the Union Address, the president set out the terms on which he would make this economic and cultural link. A year earlier in his 1995 State of the Union Address, he had been apologetic about biting off more than he could chew. No more. This time Clinton was unapologetic about the direction in which his administration was moving. "The era of big government is over," he insisted, going out of his way to "compliment the Republicans for the energy and determination they have brought to this task." It was now time to finish the job and resolve the remaining differences — not principles — that separated his budget plans from those of Congress. "We must make permanent deficits yesterday's legacy," remembering only that "we cannot go back to the time when our citizens were left to fend for themselves," the president concluded.

In the context of the State of the Union Address, the president's caveat was, however, primarily an assurance to the middle class that its interests, whether reflected in Medicare or in college tuition tax credits, would not be forgotten by his administration as they would be by the Contract with America. Paralleling the president's willingness to reduce the size of government and the aid it traditionally supplied to the poor was his desire to make government more punitive to those who in his judgment threatened social stability. By the end of his State of the Union Address, Clinton had come out in favor of time limits and "tough" work requirements for those on welfare, new laws to make sure fathers paid child support, programs to keep the teen pregnancy rate down, a V-chip in television sets to allow parents to screen out programs they believed their children should not watch, and a one-strike-and-you're-out rule for residents of public housing who committed crimes and peddled drugs.[19]

The unabashedly Republican tilt of the president's speech, with its insistence that many of the nation's problems were behavioral rather than economic, was immediately noted by the media. "Clinton Embraces GOP

Themes in Setting Agenda," the *Washington Post* observed in its January 24 banner head, and in its lead story on January 24, the *New York Times* reached the same conclusion. "Tried to Pre-empt G.O.P. Messages," the *Times* told its readers in its front-page headline. Bob Dole's Republican response to the president's address, written by Mari Will, the wife of conservative columnist George Will, took a very different line. Rather than accusing the president of taking a me-too Republican position, Dole argued that Clinton was in fact the defender of the kind of liberalism that believed there was only one answer for our problems: "More government. Bigger government. And more meddlesome government." Following the script outlined by George Bush against Michael Dukakis in 1988, Dole went on to say of the Clinton administration, "It is as though our government and our institutions and our culture have been hijacked by liberals and are careening dangerously off course." By the end of his response, Dole had put Clinton in the category of Big Brother. The president's ambitious social programs, Dole argued, threatened the country with an Orwellian nightmare.[20]

Within Dole's own party, the response to the speech was sharply critical. "The message Republicans should take away from Dole's speech," Pat Buchanan observed, "was that our pitcher got shelled and we've got to go to the bullpen if we want to win the series." Senator Phil Gramm of Texas, campaigning against Dole in Iowa, was even gloomier. "There has been a growing belief at the grassroots level in these early primary states where people are starting to pay attention that Bob Dole could not win. I think last night simply crystallized that concern," he told reporters. For Clinton, by contrast, Dole's speech was everything he could have wanted. Instead of pointing out how the reductions in government services that Clinton advocated would hurt the poor and minorities, Dole insisted that Clinton was too much of a Democrat, thus shielding the president from criticism by the left. Having been accused of being too soft and too liberal, he could continue to move to his right without having to defend himself against the charge of being hardhearted.[21]

And that is exactly what the president did from January until the Democratic National Convention in August. During this time the president called for a rise in the minimum wage from $4.25 to $5.15 an hour, came out in favor of the Kennedy-Kassebaum health bill, which allowed workers to carry their health coverage from job to job, and proposed legislation that offered tax relief for the cost of college tuition. But the president's chief advocacy during this period, in contrast to his ambitious legislative proposals of 1993 and 1994, was for a series of small-scale programs designed to enhance his standing as a defender of family values.[22]

In a series of speeches delivered at the White House and in campaign stops across the country, the president spelled out his belief that local schools should be able to require their students to wear school uniforms, approved the Anti-Terrorism and Effective Death Penalty Act limiting death-row appeals by convicted murderers, signed federal legislation requiring states to notify communities of the whereabouts of convicted child molesters when they were released from jail, let it be known that he would sign legislation allowing states to deny recognition of same-sex marriages, reasserted his belief in the V-chip, praised the use of curfews to curb teenage crime, and backed a constitutional amemdment giving crime victims the right to be heard at court proceedings involving the defendants in their cases.[23]

Liberal economist Robert Kuttner, concerned that the government was doing nothing to help the poor find work or to deal with the impact of the new global economy on falling wages, later complained, "For the first time in a century, both parties are effectively committed to the proposition that major social and economic ills are beyond government's capacity to remedy." But among voters the president's strategy of wrapping himself in family-values issues and avoiding the tough legislative fights that might have revived memories of his first two years in office was a success. In April his approval ratings continued to stand at above 50 percent, and his lead over Dole remained between 12 and 15 points. Two months later the gap had gotten even wider. A *New York Times* poll conducted between June 20 and June 23 showed the president leading Dole by 20 points, 54 percent to 34 percent. On only one issue, welfare, where twice before he had vetoed Republican-sponsored bills for being too harsh on the poor, was the president vulnerable to the charge of being overly liberal. The situation was very much like the one he had faced in the summer of 1995, when his reluctance to commit himself to a balanced budget gave the Republicans a clear-cut issue on which to attack him. But as he had done in 1995, the president moved to the right on this issue and made sure his troubles did not get worse. On July 31, despite objections from many long-time allies, including Marion Wright Edelman of the Children's Defense Fund, the president announced that he would sign the welfare bill making its way through Congress and end six decades of federal guarantees for the poor.[24]

If Bob Dole wanted to take back what was now being called the center from Bill Clinton, his only option was to reverse course and begin to moderate his own position. But instead of battling Clinton for the center, Dole continued to counter Clinton's moves to the right by moving further to the right himself and charging the president with being too liberal and, as if the 1990s were the 1950s, soft on defense. With an electorate that saw the president as being in retreat from the positions he had taken early in his administration, this was the least effective strategy for Dole to follow, and as the campaign went on, he became more and more isolated from the voters. Especially to middle-class voters, the suburban soccer moms he desperately needed, Dole's version of leaner and meaner government didn't just promise to make things tougher for the poor and minorities. With its cuts in middle-class entitlements, it now promised to make things tougher for *them*. Worse still for Dole, on a series of key cultural issues, he and the Republicans, rather than the Democrats, now seemed out of sync with the country. The Republicans' stances on gun control and abortion turned off voters they needed, and when Dole in interview after interview asserted that tobacco was not addictive, he only heightened his reputation as someone who was out of it.[25]

Desperate to come up with an issue that would give new life to his floundering campaign, on August 5, less than a week after the president announced he would sign the new welfare bill, Dole offered his own preconvention surprise: a $548 billion tax proposal designed to cut income taxes by 15 percent across the board. It was, Dole declared, an effort on his part to "finish the job Ronald Reagan started so brilliantly," and in newspapers and on television across the country, his tax proposal immediately became the lead story. Among voters, however, there was a sense that government had been made as lean and mean as it could be and that any further cuts were a gimmick. The *New York Times*, which in an editorial described the Dole proposal as "the Hail-Mary Tax Play," was not alone in its doubts. A *Washington Post*/ABC News survey showed that given a choice between balancing the budget and cutting taxes, 58 percent favored balancing the budget, and a majority, 53 percent, said that they opposed a middle-class tax cut if it would make balancing the budget more difficult.[26]

Although neither Clinton nor Dole knew it, the 1996 presidential campaign was effectively over. The voters had defined for themselves the limits to which they were prepared to go in dismantling government. They were not about to concern themselves with new proposals, as the sagging interest in both campaigns now showed. At the Republican National Convention Dole's acceptance speech drew an audience of just 17.9 million households, compared with 23.7 million for Bush in 1992, while Clinton's speech at the Democratic National Convention was watched by 19.6 million households, compared to 24.3 million four years earlier.[27]

■ ■ ■

With so much riding on the outcome, however, it was impossible for Bill Clinton or Bob Dole to pull back from the campaigns they had undertaken. At the Republican convention the GOP's frustrations were reflected in the Hillary Clinton dismemberment dolls that vendors sold for twenty dollars apiece. The rag doll with arms and legs that could be torn off, gave anyone who bought it an excuse to have a temper tantrum.[28]

The problem for the Republicans was that at this stage of the campaign it was much more difficult to pull Bill Clinton apart. Unable to attack his programs without simultaneously attacking their own core beliefs, they were forced to criticize the president personally or else claim that the real Bill Clinton was the Clinton of 1993–94. Dole's acceptance speech reflected the Republicans' dilemma. After portraying himself as "the bridge to a time of tranquility," he immediately made the president his primary target. The administration, Dole insisted, was run by a "corps of elite who never grew up, never did anything real, never sacrificed, and never learned." It was an administration easy on drugs, weak on defense, liberal in its judicial appointments, and, above all, untrustworthy. Having failed to discredit the president's coopting of the Contract with America, Dole had no other way to go after him. Dole would continue in this vein until the final day of the campaign, when at a Las Vegas rally he proclaimed, "The American people are beginning to understand that character does matter."[29]

The Republican television ads, resurrecting four-year-old MTV footage of Bill Clinton joking about marijuana, stressed the character issue, while Dole's stump speeches focused on the president as "a liberal, liberal, liberal every step of the way." If voters had perceived Clinton as a closet liberal or seen the character issue as decisive, such an attack might have worked. But by late September the polls still showed Clinton with a double-digit lead. In late August it was revealed that Dick Morris, the architect of the Democratic triangulation strategy, regularly visited a prostitute. The story gave the Republicans plenty of new ammunition, but the Morris revelations, after two weeks of sensational coverage, went nowhere. In California after Morris resigned from the Clinton campaign, Dole seemed desperate when he told reporters, "Morris has been trying to make President Clinton a Republican. Now maybe he'll revert to the liberal Democrat he is."[30]

Nor was Dole's situation any better a month later when, during the second presidential debate, he mounted a new personal attack on the president, insisting that Clinton was responsible for "scandals on almost a daily basis" and a climate in which "people have lost their faith in government." A *New York Times*/CBS poll taken days after the second presidential debate showed that Dole's personal assaults on the president only turned off voters. By the last weeks of the campaign, there was nothing more that Dole could do. In a final effort to gain a come-from-behind win in California, he tried to bring down the president's ratings by accusing him of bowing to "militant special interests" concerning illegal immigration. Eleven days later he went on the offensive again, this time playing the race card by coming out against affirmative action, drawing a distinction between his own support of California's anti-affirmative-action Proposition 209 and the president's opposition to it. With the polls remaining overwhelmingly in the president's favor, the result was, however, only more frustration for Dole. By the end the media and the voters, along with the Clinton administration, had become Dole targets. In Dallas he implored the electorate to "rise up" against the liberal biases of the media, telling them "Don't read that stuff! Don't watch television! Make up your mind!" In Florida he openly expressed his fears that nobody was listening to him any more. "I wonder sometimes what people are thinking about — if people are thinking at all," he told voters at a Pensacola Junior College rally.[31]

By contrast, the president's emphasis on family values and on leaner and meaner government continued to pay off. At the Democratic National Convention he had taken Dole's notion of being a bridge from the past and turned it around by proclaiming that he would be a bridge to the twenty-first century, and for the rest of the fall, he continued to show that he could top any Republican proposal by making it more acceptable. "It's a clear unambiguous choice about building a bridge to the future or going back to a past that didn't work the first time," the president observed at an early September rally in St. Louis, and over the next two months, he never deviated from that theme. When the Republicans sought to outflank him on crime, the president countered by proposing a $44 million fund for crime victims and arguing that teenagers should be required to pass a drug test before receiving a driver's license. When Congress passed a bill denying federal recognition and benefits to same-sex couples who marry, the president not only signed the bill, he made a point of running ads about his support for the bill on Christian radio stations in fifteen states.[32]

Even opposition within his own administration now seemed to work to the president's benefit. When two senior officials in the Department of Health and Human Services, Peter Edelman and Mary Jo Bane, resigned to protest the welfare law the president had signed in August, the point they made was one the president had been insisting on all along: he was no liberal. He was a nineties centrist, prepared to shrink the government by balancing the budget and cutting the deficit, even though that meant those at the bottom of society would be hardest hit. On November 5, just as the polls had predicted, the president swept to victory, taking the electoral college by a margin of 379 to 159 and winning eight of the ten largest states.[33]

"Two years ago not many people thought we would be here," the president told a cheering crowd of staff and supporters the day after the election. As the first Democrat since Franklin Roosevelt to win a second term, the president had every reason to take pride in what he had accomplished. Written off as politically dead two years earlier, he had correctly understood that the Republican victory of 1994 represented a historical turning point and that whoever wanted to become president in 1996 would have to base his campaign on the country's loss of faith in the kind of big government represented by the New Deal and the Great Society.[34]

If any group had a right to feel politically vindicated, as opposed to politically rewarded, by the presidential election of 1996, however, it was the losing Republicans. To be sure, the Democrats had prevented the Contract with America from being enacted along the lines its sponsors wanted, but they had done so only through a series of strategic retreats. It was the Republicans who dictated the narrow grounds on which the election was fought and the new political consensus that the 1996 election ratified. Newt Gingrich was not simply defending himself or rationalizing Bob Dole's impending defeat when he told an interviewer a month before the November vote, "We have profoundly altered the balance of power in the structure of the system" and created a politics in which Democrats "are trapped in a world they don't like, where the federal government is diminishing as the arbiter of life in America." In moving to the right after being forced to abandon the activist agenda of his first two years in office, Bill Clinton did not fundamentally challenge the Contract with America — with its emphasis on a balanced budget, deficit reduction, and minimal welfare — so much as devise a political settlement that made the Contract palatable. As conservative author Dinesh D'Souza put it, the president's winning argument was, "I, Clinton will help usher in this conservative era, but I'll do it moderately, cautiously, without letting the Republican extremists take you off the cliff."[35]

For middle-class voters — the "you" in D'Souza's description — who gave the president his margin of victory in an election in which the turnout was the lowest since 1924, it was not the kind of winning argument that aroused political passion. But it left them feeling much better than the Contract with America did. And it offered them the assurance that their interests would not be sacrificed for those of the poor or in the name of liberal abstractions. All one had to do was look at the official titles — the Anti-Terrorism and Effective Death Penalty Act, the Personal Responsibility and Work Opportunity Act, the Defense of Marriage Act — of the legislation dealing with law and order, welfare reform, and gays that the president had made such a point of signing in 1996 to see that the political costs of the new leaner and meaner government which the Clinton administration now labeled as centrist were never intended to fall on mainstream America.[36]

EPILOGUE

—

Looking Backward

IN *Looking Backward,* Edward Bellamy's classic nineteenth-century utopian novel, Julian West, a wealthy Boston Brahmin, falls asleep in a sealed room in his house on Decoration Day in 1887 and awakens from a deep trance 113 years later at the start of the next millennium. Julian's trance has kept him from aging, and, like Rip Van Winkle, he begins his new life in good health but in a state of shock. The shock soon turns to joy, however. Julian has left behind a world of social strife in which he felt, as a rich man living among the poor, as if he belonged to an alien race. The America of 2000 is by contrast a model of efficiency and egalitarianism. The government is a Great Trust for which everybody works for part of his life. The labor strikes and social unrest that caused Julian so much worry in 1887 are gone. Science and cooperative management have produced a new solidarity. Best of all, the transition to a modern utopia has been accomplished without bloodshed. As Julian's host and social guide, Dr. Leete, explains to him, "The change had been long foreseen. Public opinion had become fully ripe for it, and the whole mass of people was behind it. There was no more possibility of opposing it by force than by argument."[1]

Much closer to the year 2000 than Julian West, our own view of the coming millennium is very different from his. Nowhere is this more apparent than in the movies, where rather than learning from our mistakes or using science to improve our lives, we see ourselves doing the opposite. As we head into the twenty-first century, we imagine the meanness and cruelty of the present, magnified beyond anything we have known, coming with us. In 1995, as we reached mid-decade, three very different futuristic films — Kathryn Bigelow's *Strange Days*, Terry Gilliam's *Twelve Monkeys*, and Kevin Costner's *Waterworld* — brought home this point with a vengeance. In each film the message was unmistakable: dystopia, not utopia, is what we can look forward to.

In *Strange Days* the setting is Los Angeles in December 1999, shortly before the start of the New Year. It is a dark and smoky Los Angeles, filled with crime and violence and a population hooked on cruelty. People need bodyguards just to get by. The history of Nazi Germany is now treated as a subject for entertainment. In a nightclub the featured act is men in brown shirts burning books. But the key to this world is virtual-reality headgear that taps into the brain and touches people's feelings more deeply than anything they experience directly. The plot of

Strange Days centers around the day-to-day life of Lenny Nero. A former cop who sells virtual-reality clips for a living, Lenny, played by the English actor Ralph Fiennes, finds himself pursuing a murderer who has used a virtual-reality clip to frame him for a killing.

The plot in *Strange Days* is, however, largely a device to keep the film from grinding to a halt. The heart of the movie is the picture it offers of America days away from the year 2000. Virtual-reality headgear has become the new dope. The people who buy the clips sold by Lenny and the other dealers can get any sort of vicarious kicks they want. There is no penalty to pay for engaging in virtual crime. As Lenny tells a husband whom he is trying to persuade to buy a sex tape, "It's about forbidden fruit. I can make it happen, and you won't even tarnish your wedding ring." The tapes that bring in the big money are not, however, those that are erotic, but much kinkier ones involving murder and rape. For these, buyers will pay big money, and as Lenny pursues the man who has framed him, we are shown a cyber-sadism industry that thrives the way coke dealing once did. At the start of the new century, the vicarious thrills we want are those that give us the power of the victimizer and the terrorist.

At the end of *Strange Days*, Lenny finds the real killer and turns out to be a comparatively good guy. But as New Year 2000 is being celebrated in the film's final scenes, the underlying spirit is one of pure gloom. What we have opted for as a nation is high-tech cruelty that is a substitute for any kind of deeper caring. "What's the point? What the hell are we celebrating?" asks an anonymous caller on a radio station that Lenny is listening to. That is the movie's rhetorical question as well, and the answer it gives leaves no room for doubting its pessimism.[2]

In *Twelve Monkeys* the darkness and rubble of Los Angeles in the year 2000 have been taken to a new level. The year is 2035. Thirty-eight years earlier a lab assistant, working with deadly viruses and motivated by nothing more than a calculating genocidal hate, loosed a plague that in 1997 killed all but 1 percent of the world's population. Those who managed to survive are living underground. Wild animals now roam the cities, and people are the hunted creatures if they surface for long.

In this context James Cole, played by Bruce Willis, is sent time traveling by the scientists who rule America. They want him to find out how the plague began, and because James is their prisoner, he has little choice but to go along with their orders. The task lands James in an insane asylum, where he meets Kathryn Railly, a psychiatrist, played by Madeline Stowe, who eventually comes to believe his story of time travel. The two set out to complete James's work and, if at all possible, to stop the plague from happening. They find the answer to the cause of the plague. They even fall in love. But in contrast to a film like *The Terminator*, no one in *Twelve Monkeys* has the power to alter the world's fate; the worst happens. Gilliam's picture of America today, filled with crumbling buildings and crackpots carrying signs predicting the end of life, becomes our future. Like the child who as a time traveler in

Twelve Monkeys is able to see his adult self die, people have nothing to look forward to.

Even more important, in the end there is nothing to relieve the bleakness of underground America in 2035. The scientists who are in charge confer with James through a sphere filled with tiny television sets rather than face to face, and at every chance they get, they treat him with cruelty. When we first see him, he has been confined to a tiny cell, but in the ravaged America of 2035 being free is no bargain. Destruction has taught us nothing. An Orwellian sadism controls both public and private life.

Sadism, only of a much more primitive variety, also defines the lives of the earth's survivors in *Waterworld*. The time is the indefinite future. A new ice age has left most of the globe covered in water. Dirt is bought and sold by the ounce, as if it were gold. People either roam the sea like nomads or live crowded together on tiny atolls. As in *Twelve Monkeys*, life is brutal, and society provides no relief. What has emerged is not a world filled with Robinson Crusoes but a world in which a crude Darwinism sets the conditions of existence.

The villains in *Waterworld* are the Smokers, a gang of pirates who represent the last vestiges of a predatory industrialism. Operating from the hull of a supertanker, they attack everyone in sight who has anything they might want. Their idea of pleasure is smoking cigarettes and joyriding in the old cars they keep below the deck of their supertanker. In contrast to the Smokers stands the ecologically pure Mariner, played by Kevin Costner. The Mariner has developed gills behind his ears, and as a successful mutant he has advantages over others in the struggle to survive. But the key to the Mariner is his ability to live with nature and waste nothing. From his wind-powered ship to his filter for turning his urine into drinking water, the Mariner uses the resources at his disposal to their utmost.

He is not, however, allowed to live in the isolation he seeks. When he stops at an atoll to do some trading, he is imprisoned by its citizens because he is a mutant. A woman with a little girl who has a map of where land is tattooed on her back helps him escape, but they are soon pursued by the Smokers, who want the map for themselves. As in *Strange Days* and *Twelve Monkeys*, the plot keeps events moving, but the real issue is what we have come to after our years of evolution. The answer is not much. After an epic battle with the Smokers, the Mariner is able to guide the girl, the woman who rescued him, and a few survivors from the atoll to land. But the Mariner does not want to be with these people who imprisoned him once. After helping them get settled, he decides that roaming the seas is best for him, and, like a gunslinger in the Old West who knows he can't be a homesteader, he takes off for parts unknown. He is not about to establish a new species.[3]

■ ■ ■

What we see in the movies is not, however, very different in its pessimism and cruelty from the kinds of "realistic" scenarios we are prepared to make at present about what awaits us down the road. In February 1994 the normally sedate *Atlantic Monthly* appeared on newsstands with a cover that showed a crumpled globe on fire and above it a headline that declared in huge capital letters: THE COMING ANARCHY: NATIONS BREAK UP UNDER THE TIDAL FLOW OF REFUGEES FROM ENVIRONMENTAL AND SOCIAL DIS- ASTER. BORDERS CRUMBLE, ANOTHER TYPE OF BOUND- ARY IS ERECTED — A WALL OF DISEASE. WARS ARE FOUGHT OVER SCARCE RESOURCES, ESPECIALLY WATER, AND WAR ITSELF BECOMES CONTINUOUS WITH CRIME, AS ARMED BANDS OF STATELESS MARAUDERS CLASH WITH THE PRIVATE SECURITY FORCES OF THE ELITES. A PREVIEW OF THE FIRST DECADES OF THE TWENTY-FIRST CENTURY. The *Atlantic* headline did not exaggerate the findings in its Robert Kaplan cover story, "The Coming Anarchy." For Kaplan, the author of an earlier book on the Balkans, the chaos of West Africa, the immediate focus of his *Atlantic* article, does not stand alone. It has become "*the* symbol of worldwide demographic, environmental, and societal stress, in which criminal anarchy emerges as the real 'strategic' danger." In the 1996 book version of his *Atlantic* essay, *The Ends of the Earth: A Journey at the Dawn of the 21st Century*, Kaplan goes on to compare his findings to those of the eighteenth-century English historian Edward Gibbon, who in *The Decline and Fall of the Roman Empire* described the empire's success as a short happy period fol- lowed by wearisome centuries of violence and chaos. But the analogy to Gibbon is gratuitous, given the ruthlessness that Kaplan sees in the future as the haves of the world protect themselves from the have-nots.[4]

Kaplan's "doomsterism," to use historian Paul Kennedy's word, has been taken seriously by the Clinton administration. In a July 1994 *Boston Globe* interview, the president spoke about Kaplan's thesis in terms of America facing a future that looked "like one of those Mel Gibson Road Warrior movies." But it is the vividness of Kaplan's scenario, rather than its pessimism, that sets it apart. Among historians, doomster scenarios in which cruelty and warfare are the norm in the future have become routine in the nineties. In a 1993 *Foreign Affairs* article, "The Clash of Civilizations?" and subsequently in a book with the same title, diplomatic historian Samuel Huntington predicted a bleak future of continuous worldwide conflict based on cultural differences, and in a 1994 *London Review of Books* essay, "Why Fascism Is the Wave of the Future," scholar Edward Luttwack was equally grim, contending that growing prosperity among the elites, in combination with increasing middle-class insecurity, will provoke the same kind of political reaction that brought Hitler and Mussolini to power after World War I.[5]

In our day-to-day lives a similarly Hobbesian view of the future may be seen most dramatically in our willingness to wage economic war against the old in order to ensure that in the next century they do not take too much from the rest of the population. The war itself and the feelings it has inspired are best described by a poster that appeared several years ago: "Senior citizens are the biggest carriers of AIDS," the poster read. "Hearing Aids, Band-Aids, Rol-Aids, Walking Aids, Medicaid, and Government Aid." Beneath the writing was a drawing of a toothless old man with a Band-Aid on his bald head and a hearing aid jutting from one ear. What lies behind the poster and the resentment it embodies is fear about the future of Social Security. In 1900, 4 percent of America's population was over sixty-five. Today 13 percent are over sixty-five, and by 2013, when the first baby boomers, those born in 1947, start to retire, the percentage will jump again. By 2020 one in every six Americans, compared to today's one in eight, will be eligible for full Social Security benefits. It is a situation that will put Social Security, which currently is producing a $65 billion surplus, thanks to adjustments made to it in 1977 under Jimmy Carter and in 1983 under Ronald Reagan, in deep trouble if nothing is done to change present law. At current rates the system will run out of money by 2025, and by 2035, the year of *Twelve Monkeys*, it will be operating at a one-trillion-dollar annual deficit. The problem could not have been foreseen when Social Security began. In 1935 average life expectancy was just sixty-two — three years younger than the age at which workers now get full benefits. Today life expectancy is seventy-six, and the average worker spends 26 percent of his or her adult life in retirement, compared to just 7 percent in 1940, when payments were made to less than 1 percent of the population.[6]

"This act does not offer anyone an easy life," Franklin Roosevelt observed of Social Security in a 1938 fireside chat, and amending Social Security to match Roosevelt's description would certainly make sense in the coming years. But what has happened in the course of the nineties is something much different: a generation war that in its spitefulness makes the youth slogan of the sixties, "Never trust anyone over thirty," seem like a joke.[7]

Leading the generation war early in the decade were two twentysomething groups — Third Millennium (now primarily a New York–based Generation X think tank) and Lead or Leave (a Washington-based organization, now defunct). The political tone taken by the two groups initially was reflected in a protest led by Lead or Leave in 1993, just six months after its founding, at the Washington headquarters of the American Association of Retired Persons (AARP). As the music of Seal and Pearl Jam blasted over the boom box they had brought with them, the Lead or Leave pickets chanted:

> One, two, three, four,
> We won't take it anymore.
> Five, six, seven, eight,
> Cut the debt, 'cause we can't wait.

The immediate reason for Lead or Leave's protest was President Clinton's new budget proposals, but in targeting the AARP and driving home the differences between generations in musical tastes, Lead or Leave was bent on making a second point as well. The elderly are getting too much of our tax money. They need to be taken down a peg.[8]

A few months later, in a *Chicago Tribune* op ed patronizingly entitled "An Appeal to Grandma and Grandpa," Rob Nelson and Jon Cowan, cofounders of Lead or Leave, continued the assault. Making the assumption that grandparents were out of touch with everyone but their own generation, Nelson and Cowan outlined how well the elderly were doing compared to the young and went on to advise, "Perhaps next time you hear from the American Association of Retired Persons, you'll let them know that you talked with your grandkids and decided that you support a fair reform of Social Security. And demand they pass the word along to Congress. Otherwise, tell them you won't be renewing your membership in AARP. You'll save yourself $5 a year and a fortune in your children's future."[9]

The growing acceptance of the ideas presented by Lead or Leave and Third Millennium may be seen in the direction that current discussions about the elderly have taken in mainstream circles. As economist Peter G. Peterson puts it in his new book *Will America Grow Up Before It Grows Old?*, we are haunted by the fear of being a "nation of Floridas." Jessica Matthews, a senior fellow at the Council on Foreign Relations, has compared cleaning up the Social Security mess to cleaning up after a herd of cows in the living room and sarcastically suggested that in the future Social Security checks should be printed in red after a retiree uses up the money he or she contributed. Senator Bob Kerrey, normally a very compassionate legislator, has cast the demands of seniors in an even more sardonic light. "Please don't tell me every American over sixty-five is foraging in the alley for garbage or eating dog food," he told the *New Republic*. "They're going to Las Vegas with their COLAS — while kids don't have computers in class." And even at the National Institute of Aging, the elderly as a class have been described almost as if they were foreigners. The aging of the baby-boom generation, Richard Suzman, the director of the Office of Demography, has declared, "could have an impact on our society of equal magnitude to the tidal wave of immigration at the turn of the century."[10]

Writing on where all this is likely to end, MIT economist Lester Thurow has predicted a future in which "class warfare is apt to be defined as the young against the old, rather than the poor against the rich." As the fears of groups like Lead or Leave and Third Millennium spread, it is clear, however, that we are not going to have to wait long for that future. Granny-bashing is here, and with 41 percent of their income on average coming from the government, the elderly are enormously vulnerable. They don't even have to be confronted personally to have their money snatched away.[11]

■　　■　　■

For Julian West, the psychological impact of being trapped in a time that seems only likely to produce a meaner version of itself comes through in the last chapter of *Looking Backward*, when in a dream he finds himself transported back to the Boston he left in 1887. He is struck by the "squalor and human degradation" he encounters on the streets, but his worst shock comes at a dinner party at the home of his fiancée when he tries to explain to the guests at the table that it is possible to have a future in which meanness and class warfare are not the rule. The other guests act as if he is insane for making such remarks, and Julian finds himself feeling like "an escaped convict who dreams that he has been recaptured and brought back to his dark and reeking dungeon." As he looks at the world through the eyes of the others at the dinner table, he realizes that in the past their eyes were his eyes, and for the moment he is overcome with fear and depression.[12]

For us the feeling of being caught up in a present that seems likely to lead only to a crueler and harsher future has been more gradual than for Julian West and hence less nightmarish. But the psychological toll it has taken has, nonetheless, been enormous. Missing from American life in the 1990s is faith in what has historically been thought of as American exceptionalism: the belief that what distinguishes us from other nations is our commitment to an ideal of democratic equality and our wish to be an example, a "city upon a hill," as John Winthrop, the first governor of Massachusetts, put it in his eighteenth-century sermon "A Model of Christian Charity." By 1994 nearly one out of five Americans was thinking about moving abroad, and for those with incomes of $50,000 and more, the figure was higher — 26 percent, according to *Money* magazine. No longer believing conditions are going to improve naturally or that government can be counted on to help us (in 1992, 75 percent of Americans said they "almost never" trust the government), we rely on making it on our own as individuals, distrusting the idea of commonality. In this context the world of *Twelve Monkeys* or the rhetoric of Lead or Leave becomes our vision of the future at its most extreme — but not an aberration.[13]

In "Bowling Alone," arguably the most influential essay of the 1990s, Harvard government professor Robert Putnam has described our commitment to looking out for number one and ignoring virtually everybody else in terms of our abandonment of associations — from bowling leagues to unions to PTAs — that provide the social capital for civility. But in meaner and even more graphic terms we can see this same vision of the present and future architecturally embodied in the new walled communities, patrolled by armed guards and shielded by gates and passes, that have become part of our landscape and turned into a real estate bonanza for so many of their owners. Varying from conventional suburban developments to a community in California with a wall, a moat, and a drawbridge, these fortress villages are home to 4 million Americans and reflect a trend (between 1990 and 1995 a third of all new developments in Southern California were gated communities) in which 28 million of us now choose to live in some sort of guarded house or apartment complex.[14]

The question is how, if at all, do we move beyond such a real and symbolic fortress world and the message it delivers: I'll take care of me and mine. The hell with you. In defending *Looking Backward* against its nineteenth-century critics, Edward Bellamy observed that at certain points in history a vision of the future was often more important than practical advice. "Until we have a clear idea of what we want and are sure we want it," he wrote, "it would be a waste of time to discuss how we are to get it."[15]

Bellamy's utopian argument remains a powerful one. The point of looking into the future as he did in *Looking Backward* is not simply to give ourselves a goal to aim for. It is to give ourselves a perspective on the present that ordinary politics does not yield. Such imaginings, as the late Irving Howe observed in his 1993 essay "Two Cheers for Utopia," remind us that in a time of diminished expectations it is a terrible mistake to acquiesce to the given just because it is here.[16]

Bellamy's and Howe's defense of utopianism cannot, however, spare us from the pessimism of our own culture, in which meanness and spite seem so deeply entrenched that we imagine them playing an even greater role in our future. In the face of such pessimism, it is, as Hollywood shows, dystopia, not utopia, that emerges as the predictor of our fate. We cannot for the life of us imagine a twenty-first century in which the cruelty of twentieth-century America shocks us the way the cruelty of nineteenth-century America now does when we look back at our historical record.

NOTES

INDEX

Notes

Introduction

1. Mike Davis, *City of Quartz: Excavating the Future in Los Angeles* (New York: Vintage, 1992), pp. 232–33.
2. See Michael Tomasky, *Left for Dead: The Life, Death, and Possible Resurrection of Progressive Politics in America* (New York: Free Press, 1996), pp. 13–14.
3. Anna Quindlen, "The Politics of Meanness," *New York Times*, Nov. 6, 1994, p. A19. "The Politics of Meanness," *Christian Science Monitor*, Sept. 26, 1994, p. 18. Neal Gabler, "A Multitude of Meanness," *Los Angeles Times*, Jan. 1, 1995, p. M1. Judy Mann, "The Cost of the Politics of Meanness," *Washington Post*," Oct. 10, 1994, p. B10.
4. Colin Turnbull, *The Mountain People* (New York: Simon and Schuster, 1972), p. 289.
5. Franklin Roosevelt, Second Inaugural Address, Jan. 20, 1937. Steven A. Holmes, "Income Disparity Between Poorest and Richest Rises," *New York Times*, June 20, 1996, pp. A1, A18. James Sterngold, "Orange County Bankruptcy: The Poor Feel the Most Pain," *New York Times*, Dec. 5, 1995, pp. A1, D8.
6. Donald L. Barlett and James B. Steele, "How U.S. Policies Are Costing American Jobs," *Philadelphia Inquirer*, Sept. 8, 1996, p. A1. AT&T vice president for human resources James Meadows in Edmund L. Andrews, "Don't Go Away Mad, Just Go Away," *New York Times*, Feb. 13, 1996, p. D6.
7. Harris Wofford quoted in E. J. Dionne, *They Only Look Dead: Why*

Progressives Will Dominate the Next Political Era (New York: Simon and Schuster, 1996), p. 79.

8. Maureen Dowd, "Plagues, Comets, Values," *New York Times*, July 28, 1996, sec. 4, p. 13. Elinor Burkett, "In the Land of Conservative Women," *Atlantic Monthly*, Sept. 1996, p. 29.

9. "The Rekindled Flame," *Wall Street Journal*, July 3, 1989, p. 6. Ron K. Unz, "Immigration or the Welfare State," *Policy Review*, Fall 1994, p. 33.

10. Michael Elliott, *The Day Before Yesterday: Reconsidering America's Past, Rediscovering the Present* (New York: Simon and Schuster, 1996), p. 24.

11. Randall Lane, "It's Live, It's Brutal," *Forbes*, May 22, 1995, p. 48. Wendell Jamieson, "JFK Limo Tour a Killer Thriller," *Daily News*, Sept. 21, 1996, p. 3.

12. Michael Tomasky, *Left for Dead*, p. 195.

13. Ellen Willis, "Down with Compassion," *New Yorker*, Sept. 30, 1996, pp. 4–5.

14. William Kittredge, *Who Owns the West?* (San Francisco: Mercury House, 1996), p. 162.

1. Mean Times

1. James Bennet, "At Michigan Rally Unyielding Anger to the Brady Bill," *New York Times*, Aug. 15, 1995, p. A10.

2. Michael Kazin, *The Populist Persuasion* (New York: Basic Books, 1995), pp. 102–245.

3. Jerry Gray, "No. 2 House Speaker Refers to Colleague with Anti-Gay Slur," *New York Times*, Jan. 28, 1995, pp. A1, A8. Tom Morganthau, "Fires in the Night," *Newsweek*, June 24, 1996, pp. 29–32.

4. Eric Schmitt, "GOP Would Give Pentagon Money It Didn't Request," *New York Times*, July 5, 1995, pp. A1, A12. David S. Broder, "Less and Less for the Poor," *Washington Post*, Oct. 1, 1995, p. C7. Anna Quindlen, "The Politics of Meanness," *New York Times*, Nov. 16, 1994, p. A19. Steven Greenhouse, "Helms Takes Swipe at Clinton, Then Calls It Mistake," *New York Times*, Nov. 23, 1994, p. A19. David Strout, "Some Rightist Shows Pulled, and Debate Erupts," *New York Times*, Apr. 30, 1995, p. A28. Kenneth B. Noble, "U.S. Warns Big Retailers about Sweatshop Goods," *New York Times*, Aug. 15, 1995, p. A14. George Vescey, "The Coach Must Control Everything," *New York Times*, Nov. 19, 1995, sec. 8, p. 11. Neal Gabler, "A Multitude of Meanness," *Los Angeles Times*, Jan. 1, 1995, p. M1.

5. William S. Cohen, "Why I Am Leaving," *Washington Post*, Jan. 21, 1996, p. C7. James Fallows, *Breaking the News: How the Media Undermine*

American Democracy (New York: Pantheon Books, 1996), pp. 16–20. Steve Jacobson, "Dis Is Out of Control," *Newsday*, May 6, 1994, p. A99.

6. Richard Hofstadter, *The Paranoid Style in American Politics and Other Essays* (New York: Alfred A. Knopf, 1965), pp. 3–40. Murray Hausknecht, "Institutionalizing Meanness," *Dissent*, Fall 1995, p. 445.

7. George Bush, State of the Union Address, Jan. 28, 1992.

8. Pat Buchanan, "The Election Is about Who We Are: Taking Back the Country," *Vital Speeches of the Day*, Sept. 12, 1992, pp. 712–15.

9. Irving Kristol, "My Cold War," *National Interest*, Spring 1993, pp. 141–44.

10. Celia W. Dugger, "Police to Start New Program for the Homeless," *New York Times*, Aug. 18, 1994, p. B1. Newt Gingrich, "The Liberals' Legacy of Failure," *USA Today*, Jan. 1990, p. 15. Excerpt of remarks on victory by Gingrich, *New York Times*, Dec. 6, 1994, p. B8. Rush Limbaugh, *See, I Told You So* (New York: Pocket Books, 1994), p. 7. James Barron, "Bob Grant Is Back on the Air," *New York Times*, Apr. 30, 1996, p. B3.

11. Lewis Lapham, "Reactionary Chic," *Harper's*, Mar. 1995, p. 37. Barry Bluestone, "The Inequality Express," *American Prospect*, Winter 1995, p. 2. Mark Levinson, "Anti-Inflation Fanaticism at the Fed," *Dissent*, Winter 1995, p. 10. Stephen S. Roach, "The New Majority: White Collar Jobless," *New York Times*, Mar. 14, 1994, p. A17. Louis Uchitelle and N. R. Kleinfield, "The Price of Jobs Lost," in *The Downsizing of America* (New York: Times Books, 1996), p. 5. Kevin Phillips, *Boiling Point* (New York: Random House, 1993), p. 12.

12. Ronald Blackwell in "Does America Still Work?" *Harper's*, May 1996, p. 41. Jack Sheinkman, "Is Downsizing a Myth?" *New York Times*, Apr. 1, 1996, p. A16. Charles Wilson quoted in *Time*, Jan. 26, 1953, p. 20. Keith Bradsher, "General Motors and Union Agree to End Walkout," *New York Times*, Mar. 22, 1996, pp. A1, D4. Al Dunlap in "Does America Still Work?" *Harper's*, May 1996, pp. 36–37.

13. "CEO Compensation," *Harper's*, May 1996, p. 46. Daniel Burstein and David Kline, *Road Warriors* (New York: Dutton, 1995), p. 329. Louis Uchitelle, "1995 Was Good Year for Companies," *New York Times*, Mar. 29, 1996, pp. A1, D8.

14. Robert Reich, "Of Butchers and Bakers: Is Downsizing Good for the Economy?" *Vital Speeches of the Day*, Dec. 1, 1993, pp. 100–01. Louis Uchitelle, "The Rise of the Losing Class," *New York Times*, Nov. 20, 1994, sec. 4, pp. 1, 5.

15. Scott Adams, *The Dilbert Principle* (New York: HarperBusiness, 1996), pp. 53, 116.

16. National Insecurity Survey in *The Downsizing of America*, p. 315. John B. Judis, "Poll Position," *New Republic*, Mar. 4, 1996, p. 4. Edward

Luttwack, "Turbo-Charged Capitalism and Its Consequences," *London Review of Books*, Nov. 1995, p. 7.

17. Stephen Ansolabehere and Shanto Iyengar, *Going Negative: How Political Advertisements Shrink and Polarize the Electorate* (New York: Free Press, 1995), p. 90.

18. Fawn Brodie, *Thomas Jefferson: An Intimate History* (New York: W. W. Norton, 1974), pp. 357–75. Ansolabehere and Iyengar, *Going Negative*, p. 89. Todd Gitlin, "Blips, Bites, and Savvy Talk," in Nicolaus Mills, ed., *Culture in an Age of Money* (Chicago: Ivan R. Dee, 1990), p. 40.

19. Wilson Carey McWilliams, "The Meaning of the Election," in Gerald Pomper, ed., *The Election of 1988* (Chatham, N.J.: Chatham House, 1989), pp. 179–80.

20. Kathleen Hall Jamieson, *Dirty Politics* (New York: Oxford University Press, 1992), pp. 17–27. Tony Coelho quoted in Ruth Shalit, "The Undertaker," *New Republic*, Jan. 2, 1995, p. 24.

21. Ansolabehere and Iyengar, *Going Negative*, pp. 90–91, 121, 92, 94.

22. "Election Notebook," *Time*, Nov. 18, 1996, p. 25. Adam Clymer, "Phony Polls That Sling Mud Raise Questions over Ethics," *New York Times*, May 20, 1996, pp. A1, B7. Larry J. Sabato and Glenn R. Simpson, *Dirty Little Secrets* (New York: Times Books, 1996), pp. 245–47, 254–55, 155–57.

23. Oralandar Brand Williams and David C. Grant, "Thief Robs, Beats Civil Rights Legend," *Detroit News*, Aug. 31, 1994, p. A1. Oralandar Brand Williams and Tarak Hamada, "Capture of Beating Suspect Turns 2 Men into Heroes," *Detroit News*, Sept. 1, 1994, p. A1. James Bennet, "Sadness and Anger after a Legend Is Mugged," *New York Times*, Sept. 1, 1994, p. A16.

24. Excerpts from Farrakhan talk, *New York Times*, Oct. 17, 1995, p. A20. Farrakhan in David Maraniss, "A Clear Day, a Cloud of Contradictions," *Washington Post*, Oct. 17, 1995, p. A21. Benjamin Chavis quoted in Francis X. Clines, "Organizers Defend Role of Farrakhan in March by Blacks," *New York Times*, Oct. 13, 1995, p. A1. Jesse Jackson quoted in Henry Louis Gates, Jr., "The Charmer," *New Yorker*, Apr. 29 and May 6, 1996, p. 129. Farrakhan quoted in "Farrakhan Remarks Stir Anger," *New York Times*, Oct. 15, 1995, sec. 1, p. 12.

25. Charles Murray and Richard J. Herrnstein, *The Bell Curve* (New York: Free Press, 1996), pp. 276, 322–26. Stephen Jay Gould, "Curve Ball," *New Yorker*, Nov. 20, 1994, pp. 139–49.

26. William J. Bennett, John J. Dilulio, Jr., and John P. Walters, *Moral Poverty* (New York: Simon and Schuster, 1996), pp. 27–28. William Bennett, "A Strategy for Transforming America's Culture," *Vital*

Speeches of the Day, July 1, 1994, p. 556. William Bennett, "Moral Values," *USA Today*, Nov. 1994, p. 16. Howard Fineman, "The Virtuecrats," *Newsweek*, June 13, 1994, pp. 31–36. Robert Rector quoted in Hilary Stout, "GOP's Welfare Stance Owes a Lot to Prodding from Robert Rector," *Wall Street Journal*, Jan. 23, 1995, p. A10.

27. Christopher Lasch, *The Revolt of the Elites* (New York: W. W. Norton, 1995), p. 45. Robert Rector quoted in Stout, "GOP's Welfare Stance."

28. John L. Mica and Barbara Cubin in Robert Pear, "House Backs Bill Undoing Decades of Welfare Policy," *New York Times*, Mar. 26, 1995, p. A9.

29. Louis Fisher, "The Contract with America: What It Really Means," *New York Review of Books*, June 22, 1995, pp. 20–24. Ronald A. Feldman, "What You Can't Learn from Boys Town," *New York Times*, Dec. 13, 1994, p. A29. Douglas Besharov, "Clinton and Congress," *New York Times*, Dec. 20, 1994, p. A23.

30. Steven A. Holmes, "The Boom in Jails Is Locking Up Lots of Loot," *New York Times*, Nov. 4, 1994, sec. 4, p. 3. Rick Bragg, "Chain Gang Returns to Roads of Alabama," *New York Times*, Mar. 26, 1995, p. A16. Adam Cohen, "Back on the Chain Gang," *Time*, May 15, 1995, p. 26. Brent Staples, "The Chain Gang Show," *New York Times Magazine*, Sept. 17, 1995, p. 62. "Chain Gangs Are Halted in Alabama," *New York Times*, June 21, 1996, p. A14. Interview with Ken Jones, Mississippi Department of Corrections, June 12, 1996. Mark Costanzo and Lawrence T. White, "An Overview of the Death Penalty and Capital Trials," *Journal of Social Issues* 50 (2), 1994, p. 10.

31. "Jailhouse Tops White House As Place to Be," *Newsday*, July 5, 1993. David Frum in "A Revolution, or Business as Usual," *Harper's*, Mar. 1995, p. 50.

32. Dick Armey quoted in Steven Waldman, *The Bill: How Legislation Really Becomes Law* (New York: Penguin Books, 1995), p. 49. Robert G. Putnam, "Bowling Alone: America's Declining Social Capital," *Journal of Democracy*, Jan. 1995, p. 69. Daniel Gross, "Can't Spare That Dime," *Washington Post*, Apr. 17, 1994, p. C1. Arlene Croce, "Discussing the Undiscussable," *New Yorker*, Dec. 26, 1994/Jan. 2, 1995, pp. 54–60.

33. Dirk Johnson, "Bid to Auction Killer's Tools Provokes Disgust," *New York Times*, May 20, 1996, p. A10. Kenneth S. Stern, *A Force upon the Plain* (New York: Simon and Schuster, 1996), pp. 15–16. Michael Kelly, "The Road to Paranoia," *New Yorker*, June 19, 1995, pp. 59–75. Tom Kenworthy and George Lardner, Jr., "The Militias," *Washington Post*, May 4, 1995, p. A23.

34. Raymond Hernandez, "A Blood Sport Gets in the Blood," *New York Times*, Apr. 11, 1995, pp. B1, B4. Joe Donnelly, "A Vicious Sport,"

Washington Post, Sept. 4, 1994, pp. B1, B4. Joseph Hanania, "Cable's No-Rules Fighting Event a Hit — and a Target," *Los Angeles Times*, Apr. 7, 1995, p. F18. Dominick Dunne, "Menendez Justice," *Vanity Fair*, Mar. 1994, pp. 108–19.

35. Arthur Schlesinger, Jr., *The Cycle of American History* (Boston: Houghton Mifflin, 1986), p. 47. Arthur Schlesinger, Jr., "Election '94: Not Realignment but Dealignment," *Wall Street Journal*, Nov. 16, 1994, p. A28. E. J. Dionne, *They Only Look Dead: Why Progressives Will Dominate the Next Political Era* (New York: Simon and Schuster, 1996), pp. 12–16. Jacob Weisberg, *In Defense of Government: The Fall and Rise of Public Trust* (New York: Scribner, 1996), pp. 188–93. Michael Tomasky, *Left for Dead: The Life, Death, and Possible Resurrection of Progressive Politics in America* (New York: Free Press, 1996), pp. 186–214. Jonathan Alter and Pat Wingert, "The Return of Shame," *Newsweek*, Feb. 6, 1995, pp. 21–25.

36. Gertrude Himmelfarb, "The Victorians Get a Bad Rap," *New York Times*, Jan. 9, 1995, p. A15. Marvin Olasky, *The Tragedy of American Compassion* (Lanham, Md.: Regnery Publishing, 1992), pp. 174–75. Newt Gingrich, *To Renew America* (New York: Harper Collins, 1995), pp. 74–78. Colin Powell, *My American Journey* (New York: Random House, 1995), p. 610.

37. Amitai Etzioni quoted in Alter and Wingert, "The Return of Shame," p. 25. Christopher Hitchens, "The Death of Shame," *Vanity Fair*, Mar. 1996, p. 72. Excerpts from Clinton's speech to black ministers, *New York Times*, Nov. 14, 1993, p. A24.

38. Ruth Benedict, *The Chrysanthemum and the Sword: Patterns of Japanese Culture* (Boston: Houghton Mifflin, 1989), pp. 222–24.

39. Jerry Gray, "Congress Votes to Add Coverage for Childbirth and Mental Illness," *New York Times*, Sept. 25, 1996, p. A15. Robert Pear, "Managed Care Officials Agree to Mastectomy Hospital Stays," *New York Times*, Nov. 15, 1996, p. 30. Robert Pear, "The New Hit Men," *Newsweek*, Feb. 28, 1996, pp. 44–48. Barbara Vobejda, "Just under Half of Possible Voters Went to the Polls," *Washington Post*, Nov. 7, 1996, p. A30.

2. The New Savagery

1. Robert D. McFadden, "296 Arrested As Police Raid Cockfight in Bronx," *New York Times*, Mar. 27, 1995, pp. A1, B3.

2. Ibid., p. B3. Raymond Hernandez, "A Blood Sport Gets in the Blood," *New York Times*, Apr. 11, 1995, pp. B1, B4.

3. Luc Sante, *Low Life: Lures and Snares of Old New York* (New York: Farrar, Straus, & Giroux, 1991), p. 107.

4. Joe Donnelly, "A Vicious Sport," *Washington Post*, Sept. 4, 1994,

pp. B1, B4. Alessandra Stanley, "New York Acts to Lift Pit Bull Controls," *New York Times*, Mar. 12, 1991, p. B1. "Dog Fight Trainers Are Blamed for Missing Pets in Philadelphia," *New York Times*, Apr. 25, 1994, p. B10.

5. Melinda Blau, "Ordinary People," *New York*, Nov. 28, 1995, pp. 39–46.

6. Joseph Hanania, "Cable's No-Rules Fighting Event a Hit — and a Target," *Los Angeles Times*, Apr. 7, 1995, p. F18. Roy Goodman quoted in Dan Barry, "Promoters of Extreme Fighting Cry Uncle," *New York Times*, Nov. 18, 1995, p. 25. Dan Barry, "Not Sweet and Not a Science," *New York Times*, Nov. 26, 1995, p. E5. Randall Lane, "It's Live, It's Brutal," *Forbes*, May 22, 1995, p. 48.

7. James Brooke, "Modern-Day Gladiators Head for Denver, But the Welcome Mat Is Rolled Up," *New York Times*, Dec. 10, 1995, p. L22. John Paul Newport, "Blood Sport," *Details*, Mar. 1995, pp. 62–72.

8. Richard Hoffer, "Gritty Woman," *Sports Illustrated*, Apr. 15, 1996, pp. 56–62. Francis Rogers, "30 Women Enter Golden Gloves," *Women's News*, Apr. 1995, p. 1. Fredia Gibbs quoted in John Soet, "Meet the Most Dangerous Woman in the World," *Inside Karate*, May 1995, p. 59.

9. Nathanael West, *Miss Lonelyhearts and The Day of the Locust* (New York: New Directions, 1933), p. 177.

10. "Rough Trading," *Economist*, Oct. 22, 1994, p. 32. "True Crime Cards Thriving Despite Outrage," *New York Times*, Dec. 6, 1992, p. A44. Josh Barbanel, "Nassau County Limits Sale of Crime Trading Cards," *New York Times*, June 16, 1992, p. B5.

11. Richard Brandt, "Video Games," *Business Week*, June 14, 1993, p. 38.

12. Marc Silver, "The Rating Game," *U.S. News and World Report*, Nov. 21, 1994, pp. 91–92. Neil Straus, "Heroes in Outworld, Fighting to Save the Earth," *New York Times*, Sept. 16, 1995, p. 16. Douglas Martin, "Bombing Iraq from Broadway for a Mere 50¢," *New York Times*, Jan. 26, 1991, p. 27.

13. Lindsey Gruson, "Video Violence," *New York Times*, Sept. 16, 1993, pp. B1, B8. Daniel Cerone, "Unlikely Heroes, Very Unlikely Hit," *Los Angeles Times*, Sept. 8, 1991, p. C3.

14. Tom Shales, "The Trashification of TV," *Washington Post National Weekly Edition*, Mar. 27–Apr. 2, 1995, p. 11.

15. Joshua Gamson, "Do Ask, Do Tell," *American Prospect* (Fall 1995), p. 48. Martin Berman quoted in Elizabeth Kolbert, "Wages of Deceit: Untrue Confessions," *New York Times*, June 11, 1995, p. H29.

16. Boxing in 1895 from a review of *Dan Stuart's Fistic Carnival* by George Robinson in *New York Times Book Review*, Feb. 12, 1995, p. 22. Brooke, "Modern Day Gladiators Head for Denver," p. L22. Senator Robert

Dole quoted in Bernard Weinraub, "Senator Moves to Control Party's Moral Agenda," *New York Times*, June 1, 1995, p. A1. Jerry Gray, "Dole, in a 2nd Nod to Right, Pledges to Fight Gun Ban," *New York Times*, Mar. 18, 1995, p. A1. Katharine Q. Seelye, "Panel Reverses Vote to Ban Cop-Killer Bullets," *New York Times*, June 16, 1995, p. A23. Sam Howe Verhovek, "States Seek to Let Citizens Carry Concealed Weapons," *New York Times*, Mar. 6, 1995, p. A1

17. Sam Howe Verhovek, "Group Is Dead Serious about Killing Thugs," *New York Times*, Feb. 11, 1995, p. 7. Steven A. Holmes, "The Boom in Jails Is Looking Up," *New York Times*, Nov. 4, 1994, p. E3. Rick Bragg, "Chain Gangs to Return to the Roads of Alabama," *New York Times*, Mar. 26, 1995, p. A16. Charles Crist quoted in Alex Lichtenstein, "Chain Gang Blues," *Dissent*, Fall 1996, p. 9. Brent Staples, "The Chain Gang Show," *New York Times Magazine*, Sept. 17, 1995, p. 62. "Chain Gangs Are Halted in Alabama," *New York Times*, June 21, 1996, p. A14. Interview with Ken Jones, Mississippi Department of Corrections, June 12, 1996. Mark Costanzo and Lawrence T. White, "An Overview of the Death Penalty and Capital Trials," *Journal of Social Issues* 50 (2), 1994, p. 10. "Number of Executions in 1995 Was Most in 38 Years," *New York Times*, Dec. 6, 1995, p. A26.

18. Tom Kenworthy and George Lardner, Jr., "Militias: Growing Apace with New Gun-Control Laws," *Washington Post National Weekly Edition*, May 15–21, 1995, p. 11. James William Gibson, *Warrior Dreams* (New York: Hill and Wang, 1994), pp. 220–27. James Bennet, "At Michigan Rally, Unyielding Anger at the Brady Bill," *New York Times*, May 15, 1995, p. A10. Frank Rich, "The Rambo Culture," *New York Times*, May 11, 1995, p. A29. Michael Kelly, "The Road to Paranoia," *New Yorker*, June 19, 1995, pp. 60–75.

19. David A. Kaplan, "Bobbitt Fever," *Newsweek*, Jan. 24, 1994, pp. 52–55. Joy Behar quoted in Cynthia Heimel, "Sure, Women Are Angry," *Newsweek*, Jan. 24, 1994, p. 58. Barbara Ehrenreich, "Feminism Confronts Bobbitry," *Time*, Jan. 24, 1994, p. 74.

20. David Hinckley, "Yes, Jax'll Ax Slurs in Lyrics," *New York Daily News*, June 23, 1995, p. 4. Bruce Britt, "Hate Lyrics: Reflections of Society or Just Mean?" *Minneapolis Star Tribune*, Feb. 2, 1992, p. F1. Houston A. Baker, Jr., *Rap and the Academy* (Chicago: University of Chicago Press, 1995), p. 62. Thomas Geier, "The Killing Fields in Rap's Gangsta-Land," *U.S. News and World Report*, Mar. 24, 1997, p. 32.

21. Bushwick Bill and bell hooks quoted in Michael Marriott, "Hard-Core Rap Lyrics Stir Black Backlash," *New York Times*, Aug. 13, 1993, pp. A1, A42.

22. See Nathan McCall, "My Rap Against Rap," *Washington Post*, Nov. 14, 1993, pp. C1, C4.

23. Sarah Kerr, "Rain Man," *New York Review of Books*, Apr. 6, 1995, p. 22.

24. Ibid., p. 23.

25. See Richard Corliss, "A Blast to the Heart," *Time*, Oct. 10, 1994, pp. 76–77.

26. Frank Rich, "The Longest Year," *New York Times*, June 15, 1995, p. A31. "Is There Anyone Who Hasn't Milked the Trial of Juice?" *New York Times*, Oct. 1, 1995, p. E7.

27. Nathanael West, *The Day of the Locust*, p. 178.

3. Corporate Darwinism

1. Edmund L. Andrews, "Job Cuts at AT&T Will Total 40,000," *New York Times*, Feb. 3, 1996, pp. A1, D2. *Newsweek*, Feb. 26, 1996.

2. Andrews, "Job Cuts at AT&T," p. A1. Leonard Sloane, "Stocks Gain As New Year Starts Strong," *New York Times*, Jan. 3, 1996, p. D1. Edmund L. Andrews, "AT&T Chief, Who Cut Jobs, Defends Pay," *New York Times*, Feb. 28, 1996, p. D7. John J. Keller, "AT&T Officials Got Big Options," *Wall Street Journal*, Feb. 27, 1996, p. A1.

3. Andrew Pollack, "Bell System Breakup Opens Up Era of Great Expectations," *New York Times*, Jan. 1, 1984, p. A12. AT&T's 1947 manual quoted in Dale Russakoff and Steven Pearlstein, "Rewired: AT&T and the Era of Economic Anxiety," *Washington Post*, May 19, 1996, p. A1.

4. John D. Rockefeller quoted in Alan Trachtenberg, *The Incorporation of America* (New York: Hill and Wang, 1982), pp. 84–85. Robert Allen, Letter to all the people of AT&T, Feb. 26, 1996.

5. *AT&T Force Management Program for Management Employees: Supervisor's Guidelines*, Nov. 15, 1995. Edmund L. Andrews, "Don't Go Away Mad, Just Go Away," *New York Times*, Feb. 13, 1996, pp. D1, D6.

6. Adele Ambrose and James Meadows quoted in Andrews, "Don't Go Away Mad," pp. D1, D6. Brenda Barbour, "Downsized? Stop Scowling and Start Searching," *Washington Post*, Sept. 29, 1996, p. C5. Interview with James Meadows, Feb. 29, 1996.

7. Robert B. Reich, "How to Avoid These Layoffs?" *New York Times*, Jan. 4, 1996, p. A21. Robert B. Reich, *The Work of Nations* (New York: Alfred A. Knopf, 1991), pp. 43–57.

8. Alan Greenspan quoted in David Wessel, "Greenspan Predicts Revival of Growth," *Wall Street Journal*, July 20, 1995, p. A2. William J. McDonough, "Opening Remarks," *Economic Policy Review*, 1 (Jan. 1995), p. 1.

9. Felix Rohatyn, "Requiem for a Democrat," speech delivered at the

Babcock Graduate School of Management, Wake Forest University, Mar. 17, 1995, p. 4.

10. Stephen S. Roach, "Worker Backlash: The Dark Side of America's Productivity-Led Recovery," Morgan Stanley Report, Feb. 1996, pp. 9–18.

11. David Herbert Donald quote and layoff figures in Louis Uchitelle and N. R. Kleinfield, "The Price of Jobs Lost," in *The Downsizing of America* (New York: Times Books, 1996), pp. 9, 4–5. Bill Clinton, State of the Union Address, Jan. 23, 1996. University of Michigan Panel Study of Income Dynamics in Clay Chandler and Richard Morin, "Prosperity's Imbalance Divides U.S.," *Washington Post*, Oct. 14, 1996, p. A1.

12. David M. Gordon, *Fat and Mean: The Corporate Squeeze of Working Americans* (New York: Free Press, 1996), pp. 220–21. Strike figures and Jay Mazur quote in Steven Greenhouse, "Strikes at 50-Year Low," *New York Times*, Jan. 29, 1996, p. A12.

13. White-collar joblessness 200,000 greater than blue-collar joblessness in Stephen S. Roach, "The New Majority: White-Collar Jobless," *New York Times*, Mar. 14, 1993, sec. 4, p. 17. Uchitelle and Kleinfield, "Price of Jobs Lost," p. 5.

14. Interview with anonymous AT&T worker, Mar. 3, 1996. *New York Times* poll in *The Downsizing of America*, pp. 48–49.

15. Steven A. Holmes, "Income Disparity Between Poorest and Richest Rises," *New York Times*, June 20, 1996, pp. A1, A18. William Lawrence quoted in Trachtenberg, *Incorporation of America*, p. 81. William Graham Sumner, "The Absurd Effort to Make the World Over," and Andrew Carnegie, "Wealth," in Richard Hofstadter, *Great Issues in American History, vol. 2* (New York: Vintage Books, 1958), pp. 92–96, 88.

16. Donald L. Barlett and James B. Steele, "How U.S. Policies Are Costing American Jobs," *Philadelphia Inquirer*, Sept. 8, 1996, p. A18. Frank Abrams quoted in Reich, "How to Avoid These Layoffs?" p. A21. U.S. Senate Armed Services Committee, *Confirmation Hearings on Charles E. Wilson as Secretary of Defense*, Feb. 18, 1953.

17. Al Dunlap in "Does America Still Work?" *Harper's*, May 1996, p. 37. Al Dunlap, "Villains? Heck No," *Newsweek*, Feb. 26, 1996, p. 48. Albert J. Dunlap with Bob Andelman, *Mean Business: How I Save Bad Companies and Make Good Companies Look Great* (New York: Random House, 1996), pp. 196–98, 200–01, 56, 210, 272, 55.

18. Herbert Stein, Corporate America, Mind Your Own Business," *Wall Street Journal*, July 15, 1996, p. A12.

19. Laurie Hays, "Gerstner Is Struggling As He Tries to Change Ingrained IBM Culture," *Wall Street Journal*, May 13, 1994, pp. A1, A8.

20. Barlett and Steele, "How U.S. Policies Are Costing American Jobs,"

p. A1. Allan Sloan, "The Hit Men," *Newsweek*, Feb. 26, 1996, p. 44. Bill Bradley, *Time Present, Time Past* (New York: Alfred A. Knopf, 1996), p. 402.

21. Michael Rothbaum quoted in Barlett and Steele, "How U.S. Policies Are Costing American Jobs," p. A21.

22. Keith Bradsher, "Showdown at GM Leaves Big Issues Still Unresolved," *New York Times*, Mar. 23, 1996, p. 1. Steven Pearlstein, "New Economy Gives Work a Hard Edge," *Washington Post*, Nov. 14, 1995, pp. A1, A12. Thomas Watrous quoted in Keith Bradsher, "Skilled Workers Watch Their Jobs Migrate Overseas," *New York Times*, Aug. 28, 1995, p. A1.

23. Louis Uchitelle, "More Downsized Workers Are Returning as Rentals," *New York Times*, Dec. 1, 1996, sec. 1, pp. 1, 34. William Branigin, "White Collar Visa," *Washington Post*, Oct. 21, 1995, p. A1. Alan Downs, *Corporate Executions* (New York: Amacom, 1995), p. 44. Peter T. Kilborn, "New Jobs Lack the Old Security in a Time of Disposable Workers," *New York Times*, Mar. 15, 1993, pp. A1, A15.

24. Downs, *Corporate Executions*, p. 194.

25. Bennett Harrison, *Lean and Mean: The Changing Landscape of Corporate Power in the Age of Flexibility* (New York: Basic Books, 1994), p. 213. Gordon, *Fat and Mean*, pp. 4–7.

26. David M. Noer, "Leadership in an Age of Layoffs," *Harper's*, May 1996, p. 39.

27. Barlett and Steele, "How U.S. Policies Are Costing American Jobs," p. A19. Christopher Drew and David Cay Johnston, "Special Tax Breaks Enrich Savings of Many in the Ranks of Management," *New York Times*, Oct. 13, 1996, sec. 1, pp. 1, 14. Diana B. Henriques and David Cay Johnston, "Managers Staying Dry As Corporations Sink," *New York Times*, Oct. 14, 1996, pp. A1, A8.

28. Transcript of *60 Minutes*, Apr. 7, 1996, p. 6. Sloan, "Hit Men," p. 46. Diana B. Henriques, "Preaching but Not Practicing?" *New York Times*, Dec. 22, 1995, pp. D1, D3.

29. "CEO Compensation," *Harper's*, May 1996, p. 46. Daniel Burstein and David Kline, *Road Warriors* (New York: Dutton, 1995), p. 329. Louis Uchitelle, "1995 Was Good for Companies and Great for a Lot of CEOs," *New York Times*, Mar. 29, 1996, pp. A1, D8. Gordon, *Fat and Mean*, p. 34. Transcript of *60 Minutes*, Apr. 7, 1996, p. 5.

30. Ellen Joan Pollock, "CEO Takes On a Nun," *Wall Street Journal*, July 15, 1996, pp. A1, A7. Hays, "Gerstner Is Struggling," p. 1. Richard W. Stevenson, "Minding More Than the Bottom Line," *New York Times*, May 9, 1996, pp. D1, D21.

31. Bradley, *Time Present, Time Past*, p. 407.

32. Kenneth N. Gilpin, "Market Takes Steepest Drop Since '91," *New York Times*, Mar. 9, 1996, p. 1. Patrick McGeehan and Dave Kansas, "Jobs Data Spark 115-Point Plunge on Industrials," *Wall Street Journal*, July 8, 1996, p. C1.
33. Mayor Norman Bloch quoted in Dale Russakoff and Steven Pearlstein, "Adjusting to a 'New Normal': AT&T's Call Takes a Toll in New Jersey," *Washington Post*, Aug. 21, 1996, pp. A1, A18–19.

4. Racial Payback

1. Bob Grant quotes from Bob Herbert, "Radio Sick Shtick," *New York Times*, May 3, 1996, p. A31. James Barron, "Bob Grant Is Back on the Air," *New York Times*, Apr. 30, 1996, p. B3.
2. Robert Bruno quoted in Barron, "Bob Grant Is Back," p. B3.
3. Kevin Sack, "Links Sought in Epidemic of Terror," *New York Times*, May 21, 1996, p. A12. Tom Morganthau, "Fires in the Night," *Newsweek*, June 24, 1996, pp. 29–32. Michael Kelly, "Playing with Fire," *New Yorker*, July 15, 1996, pp. 28–35. Peter Applebome, "From Atlanta to Birmingham, Blur of Progress and Stagnation," *New York Times*, Aug. 3, 1994, p. A14.
4. Thomas B. Edsall, "Rights Drive Said to Lose Underpinnings," *Washington Post*, Mar. 9, 1991, p. A6.
5. Cornel West quoted in Peter Applebome, "Rights Movement in Struggle for an Image as Well as a Bill," *New York Times*, Apr. 3, 1991, p. A1.
6. National Science Survey in Richard Morin, "Racism Knows No Party Lines," *Washington Post National Weekly Edition*, Sept. 20–26, 1993, p. 37.
7. *Washington Post*, Kaiser Family Foundation, and Harvard University Survey in Richard Morin, "A Distorted Image of Minorities: Poll Suggests That What Whites Think They See May Affect Beliefs," *Washington Post*, Oct. 8, 1995, p. A1.
8. Tom Incantalupo, "Texaco Settles," *Newsday*, Nov. 16, 1996, p. A27. Kurt Eichenwald, "The Two Faces of Texaco," *New York Times*, Nov. 10, 1996, sec. 3, pp. 1, 10. Robert Ulrich and Richard Lundwall quoted in Jack E. White, "Texaco's White-Collar Bigots," *Time*, Nov. 18, 1996, p. 104.
9. Don Terry, "Inner City Math Exam Stirs Anger," *New York Times*, May 25, 1994, p. B8. Richard Kraft quoted in Matt Bai, "Yankee Imperialists," *New York*, July 25, 1994, pp. 34–35.
10. "Bigotry Under the Boards," *Brown Alumni Monthly*, March 1996, p. 16. Applebome, "From Atlanta to Birmingham," p. A14. David

Stout, "Dismayed Greenwich Confronts a Message of Hate in Year-book," *New York Times*, June 15, 1995, p. B1.

11. Richard J. Herrnstein and Charles Murray, *The Bell Curve* (New York: Free Press, 1996), pp. 272–315.

12. Jared Taylor, *Paved with Good Intentions: The Failure of Race Relations in Contemporary America* (New York: Carroll and Graf, 1992), p. 331. Dinesh D'Souza, *The End of Racism* (New York: Free Press, 1995), p. 16. Katharine Q. Seelye, "Republicans Change Portrait and Democrats Are Furious," *New York Times*, Jan. 25, 1995, p. A15.

13. Taylor, *Paved With Good Intentions*, p. 301. Stephen Glass, "Taxis and the Meaning of Work," *New Republic*, Aug. 5, 1996, pp. 20–23. Linda Chavez, "What to Do about Immigration," *Commentary*, Mar. 1995, p. 35.

14. Bill Clinton and Al Gore, *Putting People First* (New York: Times Books, 1992), p. 164. Mickey Kaus, "They Blew It," *New Republic*, Dec. 6, 1994, p. 18.

15. Murray Hausknecht, "Institutionalizing Meanness," *Dissent*, Fall 1995, p. 445.

16. Jesse Jackson quoted in Richard Cohen, "Common Ground on Crime," *Washington Post*, Dec. 21, 1993, p. A23. Ed Koch, "Blacks, Jews, Liberals, and Crime," *National Review*, May 16, 1994, p. 36. Bill Bradley, "The Real Lessons of L.A.," speech to the U.S. Senate, Mar. 26, 1992.

17. Roger Morris, *Partners in Power: The Clintons and Their America* (New York: Henry Holt, 1996), p. 465. Brent Staples, "The Chain Gang Show," *New York Times Magazine*, Sept. 17, 1995, p. 62. Rick Bragg, "Chain Gangs to Return to Roads of Alabama," *New York Times*, Mar. 26, 1995, p. A16.

18. Andrew Hacker, "Goodbye to Affirmative Action," *New York Review of Books*, July 11, 1996, p. 24.

19. Poll in *Newsweek*, Apr. 3, 1995, p. 25. Justice Harry Blackmun in *Regents of the University of California v. Bakke*, June 28, 1978.

20. D'Souza, *The End of Racism*, p. 335. Lino A. Graglia, "Affirmative Discrimination," *National Review*, July 5, 1993, p. 28.

21. Drummond Ayres Jr., "Foes of Affirmative Action Claim California Ballot Spot," *New York Times*, Feb. 22, 1996, p. A14. Sam Howe Verhovek, "Vote in California Is Motivating Foes of Anti-Bias Plans," *New York Times*, Nov. 10, 1996, p. A1. Bob Dole, "Remarks on Affirmative Action," Oct. 28, 1996. Adam Nagourney, "Dole Sees Failure of Three Decades in Anti-Bias Fight," *New York Times*, Oct. 29, 1996, pp. A1, A21.

22. Justice Joseph Bradley in *The Civil Rights Cases*, Oct. 15, 1883.

23. Justice Sandra Day O'Connor in *Adarand Constructors v. Pena*, June 12, 1995. Linda Greenhouse, "Justices, 5 to 4, Cast Doubts on U.S. Programs That Give Preferences Based on Race," *New York Times*,

June 13, 1995, pp. A1, D25. Drew S. Days III, "Fullilove," *Yale Law Journal,* Jan. 1987, pp. 453–85.

24. Justice Anthony Kennedy in *Miller v. Johnson,* June 29, 1995. Linda Greenhouse, "Justices, in 5–4 Vote, Reject Districts Drawn with Race as the Predominant Factor," *New York Times,* June 30, 1995, pp. A1, A23. Steven A. Holmes, "Voting Rights Experts Say Challenges to Political Map Could Cause Turmoil," *New York Times,* June 30, 1995, p. A23. Cynthia McKinney quoted in Carol M. Swain, "The Future of Black Representation," *American Prospect,* Fall 1995, p. 78. Linda Greenhouse, "High Court Voids Race-Based Plan for Redistricting," *New York Times,* June 14, 1996, pp. A1, A24.

25. Judge Jerry E. Smith of the Fifth Circuit quoted in Jeffrey Rosen, "The Day the Quotas Died," *New Republic,* Apr. 22, 1996, p. 24. Julian Bond quoted in William Douglas, "Blacks Finding Less Promise in Political World," *Cleveland Plain Dealer,* Dec. 28, 1995, p. A2.

26. Chief Justice William Rehnquist in *Board of Education of Oklahoma City v. Robert Dowell,* Jan. 15, 1991.

27. Chief Justice William Rehnquist in *Missouri v. Jenkins,* June 12, 1995. Linda Greenhouse, "Justices Say Making States Pay in Desegregation Case Was Error," *New York Times,* June 13, 1995, pp. A1, D25. William Cellis III, "Forty Years after Brown, Segregation Persists," *New York Times,* May 18, 1994, p. A1. Mary Jordan, "In Cities Like Atlanta, Whites Are Passing on Public Schools," *Washington Post,* May 24, 1993, pp. A1, A12. James S. Kunen, "The End of Integration," *Time,* Apr. 29, 1996, pp. 39–45.

28. Martin Luther King, Jr., *Where Do We Go From Here: Chaos or Community?* (New York: Harper and Row, 1967), p. 49.

29. Michael Janofsky, "Debates on March and Farrakhan Persist As Black Men Converge on the Capital," *New York Times,* Oct. 16, 1995, p. A7. Phillip M. Richards, "Farrakhan's Middle-Class Revival Comes to Howard," *Dissent,* Spring 1996, p. 84.

30. Excerpts from Farrakhan talk, *New York Times,* Oct. 17, 1995, p. A20.

31. David Rieff, "The Case Against Sensitivity," *Esquire,* Nov. 1990, p. 120. Martin Gottlieb, "Mandela's Visit, New York's Pride," *New York Times,* June 24, 1990, p. E1.

32. Jim Sleeper, "The Decline and Rise of Bigotry," *Cosmopolitan,* June 1994, p. 208. "Furor Erupts over Malcolm X Mural," *Washington Post,* May 22, 1994, p. A15. Ellis Cose, *The Rage of a Privileged Class* (New York: Harper Collins, 1993), p. 144. Anthony DePalma, "Separate Ethnic Worlds Grow on Campus," *New York Times,* May 18, 1991, pp. 1, 7. "Blacks Form Graduation Panel of Their Own," *New York Times,* Feb. 17, 1991, p. 1.

33. "All in the Family," *New Republic*, Jan. 24, 1994, pp. 6–7. NABSW quoted in Julie C. Lythcott-Haims, "Where Do Mixed Babies Belong?" *Harvard Civil Rights–Civil Liberties Law Review*, Summer 1994, p. 555. Randall Kennedy, "Kids Need Parents — of Any Race," *Wall Street Journal*, Nov. 9, 1993, p. A18. Randall Kennedy quoted in Sleeper, "The Decline and Rise of Bigotry," p. 209.

34. Brent Staples, *Parallel Time: Growing Up in Black and White* (New York: Pantheon Books, 1994), pp. 202–4. Peter Applebome, "Rise Is Found in Hate Crimes Committed by Blacks," *New York Times*, Dec. 13, 1993, p. A12. Los Angeles riot quotes in Jennifer L. Hochschild, *Facing Up to the American Dream* (Princeton: Princeton University Press, 1995), p. 211. Eric Pooley, "Capitalizing on a Killer," *New York*, Apr. 18, 1994, pp. 38–39. Jim Sleeper, "Psycho-Killer," *New Republic*, Jan. 10 and 17, 1994, p. 18. William Neuman, "Khalid Salutes the LIRR Gunman," *New York Post*, Apr. 21, 1994, p. 3.

35. Henry Louis Gates, Jr., "Thirteen Ways of Looking at a Black Man," *New Yorker*, Oct. 23, 1996, p. 65. Jeffrey Rosen, "The Bloods and the Crits," *New Republic*, Dec. 9, 1996, pp. 27–42. See also Jeffrey Toobin, *The Run of His Life: The People v. O.J. Simpson* (New York; Random House, 1996), pp. 424–38. Paul Butler, "Racially Based Jury Nullification: Black Power in the Criminal Justice System," *Yale Law Journal*, Dec. 1995, pp. 677–725.

36. John F. Kennedy, Radio and television report to the American people on civil rights, June 11, 1963.

5. Lifeboat Ethics and Immigration Fears

1. Ramona Ripston quoted in Eric Malnic and Edward J. Boyer, "Deputies Clubbing of Two Suspects Taped," *Los Angeles Times*, Apr. 2, 1996, p. A1. Julia Preston, "Beating Increases Tension on Immigration," *New York Times*, Apr. 6, 1996, p. 10.

2. Tom Gorman, "Riverside Deputies to Hold Their Own Rally," *Los Angeles Times*, Apr. 11, 1996, p. A3. Kenneth B. Noble, "Sympathies Sharply Divided On Beatings of Two Immigrants," *New York Times*, May 6, 1996, p. A10. Mayor Lenwood Long quoted in Joe Vargo, "Cities Tell Reaction to Beating Incident," *Press Enterprise*, Apr. 4, 1996, p. B1.

3. Mark Mellman quoted in Ronald Brownstein and Richard Simon, "The Great Divide," *Los Angeles Times*, Nov. 14, 1993, p. A1.

4. Alan C. Miller, "Data Sheds Heat, Little Light, on Immigration Debate," *Los Angeles Times*, Nov. 21, 1993, p. A26.

5. "Don't Panic," *New Republic*, Nov. 21, 1994, p. 7. Hanna Rosin, "Raisin' Hell," *New Republic*, Nov. 14, 1994, pp. 15–16.

6. Dale Maharidge, *The Coming White Minority: California's Eruptions and the Nation's Future* (New York: Random House, 1996), pp. 142, 168. Drummond Ayers, Jr., "Anti-Alien Sentiment Spreading in Wake of California Measure," *New York Times*, Dec. 4, 1994, pp. 1, 42. Drummond Ayers, Jr., "California Governor Seeking Identification Cards for All," *New York Times*, Oct. 27, 1994, p. A1, A27. Times Poll, *Los Angeles Times*, Nov. 10, 1994, p. B2.

7. "Where They Stand," *Los Angeles Times* (reprint edition), Nov. 14–30, 1993, p. 21.

8. Eric Schmitt, "House Approves Ending Schooling of Illegal Aliens," *New York Times*, Mar. 21, 1996, p. D25. Yankelovich poll in *Time* (Fall 1993), pp. 10–12. Times Mirror Center poll in Roy Beck, *The Case Against Immigration* (New York: W. W. Norton, 1996), p. 30. Roper poll in Roy Beck, "The Pro-Immigration Lobby," *New York Times*, Apr. 30, 1996, p. A21.

9. William Knight and anti-immigrant ditty in Dan Morain and Mark Gladstone, "Racist Verse Stirs Up Anger," *Los Angeles Times*, May 19, 1993, p. A3. Maharidge, *The Coming White Minority*, p. 160. Anna Deavere Smith, *Twilight: Los Angeles, 1992* (New York: Anchor Books, 1992), p. 175. Thomas Fleming, "The Real American Dilemma," *Chronicles*, March 1989, p. 11.

10. *American Heritage*, Mar. 1994. Pat Buchanan quoted in *New York Times*, Mar. 25, 1996, p. A15. Peter Brimelow, *Alien Nation: Common Sense about America's Immigration Disaster* (New York: Random House, 1995), pp. 122, 130–31, 63. Lothrop Stoddard, *The Rising Tide of Color* (New York: Charles Scribner's, 1920), p. 303.

11. John O'Sullivan, "America's Identity Crisis," *National Review*, Nov. 21, 1994, p. 41. George Kennan, *At a Century's Ending: Reflections 1982–1995* (New York: W. W. Norton, 1996, p. 114.

12. "The Ad Campaign," *New York Times*, June 22, 1996, p. 8. "The Ad Campaign," *New York Times*, June 27, 1997, p. A20.

13. Sam Howe Verhovek, "A 2,000 Mile Fence? First, Get Estimates," *New York Times*, Mar. 3, 1996, sec. 4, p. 1. Stephen Chapman, "Birth Control," *New Republic*, Apr. 8, 1996, pp. 11–14. Eric Schmitt, "English as Official Language Wins Backing of House Panel," *New York Times*, July 25, 1996, p. A18. Mark Falcoff, "Our Language Needs No Law," *New York Times*, Aug. 5, 1996, p. A17.

14. Mike Royko, "Endorsement of Week Is Not Meant for Weak," *Chicago Tribune*, Feb. 27, 1996, p. N3.

15. Aaron Bernstein, "Huddled Masses Yearning for Your Job?" *Business Week*, Apr. 22, 1996, p. 15. Nicolaus Mills, "The Era of the Golden

Venture," in Mills, ed., *Arguing Immigration* (New York: Simon and Schuster, 1994), pp. 15–16.

16. John Kennedy, White House press release, July 23, 1963, in *Department of State Bulletin*, Aug. 19, 1963, p. 298. Lyndon Johnson, Remarks at the signing of the immigration bill, Oct. 3, 1965.

17. Edward Kennedy quoted in Tom Morganthau, "America: Still a Melting Pot?" *Newsweek*, Aug. 9, 1993, p. 21. Robert Kennedy quoted in George J. Borjas, *Friends or Strangers: The Impact of Immigrants on the U.S. Economy* (New York: Basic Books, 1990), p. 32.

18. Borjas, *Friends or Strangers*, p. 31. Mills, "The Era of the Golden Venture," p. 17. Lamar Smith, "Scare Talk about Immigration Reform," *Washington Post*, Oct. 18, 1995, p. A19. Beck, *The Case Against Immigration*, p. 15. Steven A. Holmes, "Census Sees a Profound Ethnic Shift in U.S." *New York Times*, Mar.14, 1996, p. A16.

19. Letter from thirty-five congressmen quoted in William Branigin, "Senator Simpson Offers Overhaul of Legal, Illegal Immigration," *Washington Post*, Nov. 4, 1995, p. A8. George J. Borjas, "Nine Immigration Myths," *National Review*, Apr. 17, 1995, p. 46. Tom Wicker, *Tragic Failure: Racial Integration in America* (New York: William Morrow, 1996), p. 82.

20. Morganthau, "America: Still a Melting Pot?" pp. 20–21. Peter D. Salins, "Take a Ticket," *New Republic*, Dec. 27, 1993, p. 13. Deborah Sontag, "Illegal Aliens Put Uneven Load on States, Study Says," *New York Times*, Sept. 15, 1994, p. A14. Steven A. Holmes, "California Governor Sues U.S. For Cost of Imprisoning Aliens," *New York Times*, Mar. 16, 1996, p. A14.

21. Barbara Vobejda, "Poor Americans Are Seen Fleeing Some States As Immigrants Move In," *Washington Post*, Sept. 12, 1993, p. A3.

22. William Branigin, "White Collar Visas: Importing Needed Skills or Cheap Labor," *Washington Post*, Oct. 21, 1995, pp. A1, A16. Robert DeMoss III, "New Rules on Immigration," *Nation's Business*, Sept. 1995, pp. 35–37. Norman Matloff, "Debugging Immigration," *National Review*, Oct. 9, 1995, p. 29. Leslie Helm, "Creating High-Tech Sweatshops," *Los Angeles Times*, Nov. 15, 1993, pp. A1, A17.

23. Cesar Chavez quoted in Michael Lind, "Smear Tactics," *New Republic*, Apr. 29, 1996, p. 42. Beck, *The Case Against Immigration*, pp. 75, 113–20. Richard Rothstein, "Immigration Dilemmas," in Mills, ed. *Arguing Immigration*, pp. 59–60. Sharon Begley, "The New Sweatshops," *Newsweek*, Sept. 10, 1990, pp. 50–52.

24. Frederick Douglass, *The Life and Times of Frederick Douglass* (1881, amended in 1892; reprint, New York: Collier Books, 1962), p. 298. William Julius Wilson, *When Work Disappears: The World of the New*

Urban Poor (New York: Alfred A. Knopf, 1996), pp. 130–32. Roger Waldinger, *Still the Promised City?* (Cambridge: Harvard University Press, 1996), pp. 7, 137–73. Lyndon Johnson, "To Fulfill These Rights," June 4, 1965. Lawrence R. Fuchs, "A Negative Impact of Affirmative Action," *Washington Post National Weekly Edition*, Feb. 20–26, 1995, p. 25. Andrew Hacker, "Goodbye to Affirmative Action?" *New York Review of Books*, July 11, 1996, p. 26.

25. Yankelovich–*New Yorker* survey in Jervis Anderson, "Black and Blue," *New Yorker*, Apr. 29 and May 6, 1996, p. 64. Jack Miles, "Blacks v. Browns," in Mills, ed., *Arguing Immigration*, pp. 114–16. Peter H. Schuck, "The New Immigration and the Old Civil Rights," *American Prospect*, Fall 1993, p. 104. Terry Anderson, "The Culture Clash in South-Central L.A.," *Los Angeles Times*, May 29, 1996, p. B9.

26. William Safire, "Self-Deportation?" *New York Times*, Nov. 21, 1994, p. A15. John Higham quoted in Brownstein and Simon, "The Great Divide," p. 1.

27. Eric Schmitt, "Bill Tries to Balance Concerns on Immigration," *New York Times*, Sept. 29, 1996, sec. 1, p. 28. Eric Pianin and Helen Dewar, "Immigration, Budget Agreement Reached," *Washington Post*, Sept. 29, 1996, pp. A1, A14.

28. "Points of Disagreement, and Agreement, on the Welfare Bill," *New York Times*, Aug. 1, 1996, p. A22. Lamar Smith quoted in Robert Pear, "Agreements Struck on Most Elements for Welfare Bill," *New York Times*, July 30, 1996, p. A10. U. S. Department of Justice, *1992 Statistical Yearbook of the Immigration and Naturalization Service* (Washington, D.C.: Government Printing Office, 1993), pp. 124–25.

6. Sexual Warfare and the Post-Liberated Man

1. Barbara Lippert, "Brut Force," *Adweek*, July 12, 1993, p. 36.

2. Gallup poll in Ellis Cose, *A Man's World* (New York: HarperCollins, 1995), p. 27. Rush Limbaugh, *The Way Things Ought to Be* (New York: Pocket Star Books, 1993), p. 194. Nicholson Baker, *The Fermata* (New York: Vintage Books, 1995). Susan Faludi, *Backlash: The Undeclared War Against American Women* (New York: Crown, 1991).

3. Susan Estrich, "The Last Victim," *New York Times Magazine*, Dec. 18, 1994, pp. 54–55. Thomas B. Edsall, "Masculinity on the Run," *Washington Post*, Apr. 30, 1995, pp. C1, C2.

4. Edsall, "Masculinity on the Run," p. C2. David A. Kaplan, "Bobbitt Fever," *Newsweek*, Jan. 24, 1994, pp. 52–55. Barbara Ehrenreich, "Feminism Confronts Bobbittry," *Time*, Jan. 24, 1994, p. 74.

5. Cynthia Heimel, "The Shame of Male Bashing," *Playboy*, Nov. 1994, p. 40.

6. Sherri Paris, "In Bed with Rush Limbaugh," *Tikkun*, Mar.–Apr. 1995, p. 33. Rush Limbaugh, *See, I Told You So* (New York: Pocket Star Books, 1994), pp. 222, 225, 226.

7. Limbaugh, *See, I Told You So*, p. 233.

8. Limbaugh, *Way Things Ought to Be*, pp. 188, 194.

9. Ibid., pp. 194, 197.

10. Ibid., p. 203.

11. Warren Farrell, *The Myth of Male Power* (New York: Simon and Schuster, 1993), pp. 11–13.

12. Ibid., pp. 15–16.

13. Dan Quayle, "Restoring Basic Values," speech delivered at the Commonwealth Club of California, May 19, 1992. Tom Shales, "Murphy Brown's Quayle Shoot," *Washington Post*, Sept. 22, 1992, p. B1. Barbara Dafoe Whitehead, "Dan Quayle Was Right," *Atlantic*, Apr. 1993, pp. 47–50.

14. Faludi, *Backlash*, pp. 304–12.

15. Robert Bly, *Iron John* (Reading, Mass.: Addison Wesley, 1990; reprint, New York: Vintage Books, 1992), pp. 2–3, 25, 63.

16. Lance Morrow, "Men, Are They Really That Bad?" *Time*, Feb. 14, 1994, p. 54.

17. Ibid., pp. 54, 56, 58.

18. Ibid., p. 55.

19. Harry Stein, "The Post-Sensitive Man Is Coming!" *Esquire*, May 1994, p. 58.

20. Ibid., pp. 59, 58.

21. Ibid., p. 59.

22. Ibid., p. 58. Michael Segell, "The Second Coming of the Alpha Male," *Esquire*, Oct. 1996, pp. 75–81.

23. Garrison Keillor, *The Book of Guys* (New York: Viking, 1993), p. 11.

24. Ibid., pp. 12, 15.

25. Ibid., pp. 23–40, 213–24, 317–40.

26. David Mamet, *Oleanna* (New York: Vintage Books, 1993), p. 65.

27. Ibid., pp. 19, 25, 47.

28. Ibid., pp. 67, 71, 73.

29. Ibid., pp. 79, 78.

30. David Mamet quoted in Bruce Weber, "Mamet: Hearings Prompted Oleanna," *Chicago Tribune*, Nov. 12, 1992, p. 15G. Michael Crichton, *Disclosure* (New York: Ballantine Books, 1993), p. 117.

31. Crichton, *Disclosure*, pp. 194–95.

32. Ibid., pp. 269, 487.

7. Reporting with Attitude

1. Maureen Dowd, "Whereas He Is an Old Boy, If a Young Chief, Honor Him," *New York Times*, June 9, 1994, p. A1.

2. See Jacob Weisberg, "Why Bill Clinton Is a Great American President, No, Really," *New York*, Sept. 5, 1994, p. 20.

3. Maureen Dowd quoted in James Fallows, *Breaking the News* (New York: Pantheon, 1996), p. 64. Clinton press secretary Michael McCurry on "gotcha atmosphere" quoted in Ken Auletta, "Inside Story: Why Did Both Candidates Despise the Press?" *New Yorker*, Nov. 18, 1996, p. 60.

4. "Clinton Suck-Up Watch," *New Republic*, Mar. 29, 1993, p. 10; May 3, 1993, p. 10; Aug. 2, 1993, p. 8; Apr. 10, 1994, p. 11.

5. Michael Duffy, "That Sinking Feeling," *Time*, June 7, 1993, pp. 23–28.

6. Stanley W. Cloud, "Clinton vs. the Press," and Michael Kramer, "He Ain't Dead Yet," *Time*, June 7, 1993, pp. 28–29.

7. Joe Klein, "What's Wrong?" *Newsweek*, June 7, 1996, pp. 17–19.

8. Michael Kelly, "Saint Hillary," *New York Times Magazine*, May 23, 1993, pp. 22, 64–65.

9. Katherine Boo, "The New Writer's Bloc," *Washington Monthly*, Nov. 1992, pp. 40. Maureen Dowd, "We Are the President," *New York Times Magazine*, Jan. 23, 1994, p. 18.

10. Nicholas Lemann, "Hope Against Hope," *New Republic*, Mar. 13, 1995, p. 32.

11. Elizabeth Drew, *On the Edge: The Clinton Presidency* (New York: Simon and Schuster, 1994), pp. 24, 47, 165.

12. Ibid., pp. 94, 67–68.

13. Ibid., pp. 96–97.

14. Ibid., pp. 420, 241, 247, 239, 424.

15. Todd Gitlin, "Blips, Bites, and Savvy Talk," in Nicolaus Mills, ed., *Culture in an Age of Money* (Chicago: Ivan R. Dee, 1990), pp. 30–35. Kathleen Hall Jamieson, *Dirty Politics* (New York: Oxford University Press, 1992), pp. 10–11. Boo, "The New Writer's Bloc," pp. 36–41.

16. Michiko Kakutani, "Opinion vs. Reality in an Age of Pundits," *New York Times*, Jan. 28, 1994, p. C1.

17. James Atlas, "When Fact Is Treated As Fiction," *New York Times*, July 24, 1994, sec. 4, p. 5. Weisberg, "Why Bill Clinton Is a Great American President," p. 20.

18. James Wolcott, "Hear Me Purr," *New Yorker*, May 20, 1996, pp. 58–59. Taylor Branch, "Clinton Without Apologies," *Esquire*, Sept. 1996, p. 171.

19. Fallows, *Breaking the News*, pp. 63–65. E. J. Dionne, *They Only Look Dead: Why Progressives Will Dominate the Next Political Era* (New York: Simon and Schuster, 1996), pp. 253–58.

20. David Maraniss, *First in His Class: A Biography of Bill Clinton* (New York: Simon and Schuster, 1995), p. 9. James B. Stewart, *Blood Sport: The President and His Adversaries* (New York: Simon and Schuster, 1996), pp. 430–31.

21. Larry Reibstein, "End of the Game," *Newsweek*, July 29, 1996, pp. 74–77.

22. Joe Klein, *Primary Colors: A Political Novel* (New York: Random House, 1996), pp. 3, 17.

23. Gene Lyons, "Anything Goes," *New York Review of Books*, Apr. 8, 1996, p. 25.

24. Richard Reeves, *Running in Place: How Bill Clinton Disappointed America* (Kansas City: Andrews and McMeel, 1996), p. 36. Camille Paglia, "Ice Queen, Drag Queen," *New Republic*, Mar. 4, 1996, p. 25.

25. Todd Purdum, "Facets of Clinton," *New York Times Magazine*, May 19, 1996, pp. 36–41.

26. David Brock, "Living with the Clintons," *American Spectator*, Jan. 1994, pp. 18–30.

27. Richard Morris, *Partners in Power: The Clintons and Their America* (New York: Henry Holt, 1996), pp. 3–7, 280, 275, 469, 441, 440, 410–13.

28. Gary Aldrich, *Unlimited Access: An FBI Agent Inside the Clinton White House* (Washington, D.C.: Regnery, 1996), pp. 12, 13, 40, 35, 102–3.

29. Ibid., pp. 137–38.

30. Maureen Dowd, "Aldrich Aims," *New York Times*, June 30, 1996, sec. 4, p. 15. Suzanne Garment, "The Disestablishment: Is Counterculture Now in Charge?" *Los Angeles Times*, July 7, 1996, p. M1. John H. Fund, "White House Insecurity," *Wall Street Journal*, June 28, 1996, p. A8. Neil A. Lewis, "Former FBI Agent Recounts Activities at the White House," *New York Times*, June 30, 1996, p. 16. David Brock quoted in Michael Isikoff and Daniel Klaidman, "Colliding Cultures," *Newsweek*, July 8, 1996, p. 28. Gary Aldrich quoted in Howard Kurtz and Michael Weisskopf, "Ex-Agent Retreats on Clinton Charge," *Washington Post*, July 1, 1996, pp. A1, A6.

31. Kurtz and Weisskopf, "Ex-Agent Retreats," *Clinton Charge*, p. A1.

32. Fallows, *Breaking the News*, pp. 66–67.

33. Richard Gooding, "Clinton Aide Kept Mistress 15 Years," *Star*, Sept. 17, 1996, p. 5. Matthew Cooper, "The Morris Meltdown," *Newsweek*, Sept. 9, 1996, pp. 32–37. Richard Lacayo, "Skunk at the Family Picnic," *Time*, Sept. 9, 1996, pp. 25–30. Stephen A. Holmes, "Dick Morris's Behavior, and Why It's Tolerated," *New York Times*, Sept. 8, 1996, sec. 4, p. 5. Chris Matthews quoted on *Good Morning America*, Sept. 17, 1996. Auletta, "Inside Story," pp. 44–60.

34. "Klein, Not Klein," *New Yorker*, July 29, 1996, p. 24. Donald Foster,

"Primary Culprit: Who Is Anonymous?" *New York*, Feb. 26, 1996, pp. 50–57. Richard Turner, "Liar's Poker," *New York*, July 29, 1996, pp. 12–13. Michael Gross, "Joe Klein's Year," *GQ*, Dec. 1996, p. 78. David Streitfeld, " 'Anonymous' Undone by His Own Hand," *Washington Post*, July 17, 1996, pp. A1, A7.

35. Larry Reibstein, "End of the Game," pp. 74–75. Leon Wieseltier, "Live and Let Die," *New Republic*, Aug. 12, 1996, p. 42. Joe Klein quoted in "Klein, Not Klein," p. 24.

8. The Contract of 1996

1. Remarks by the president at the White House correspondents' dinner, May 8, 1996.

2. Garry Wills, "One Sings, the Other Doesn't," *New York Times*, May 14, 1996, p. A23.

3. Scott Reed quoted in Howard Fineman and Mark Hosenball, "Dishing Dirt," *Newsweek*, May 20, 1996, p. 27. Ann Lewis quoted in Michael Kelly, "This Year's Model," *New Yorker*, June 17, 1996, p. 47.

4. Wilson Carey McWilliams, *The Politics of Disappointment: American Elections, 1976–1994* (Chatham, N.J.: Chatham House Publishers, 1995), p. 66. James Bennet, "Who's a Centrist? Clinton According to Helms Ad," *New York Times*, Oct. 3, 1996, p. A20. Adam Clymer, "For G.O.P. Freshman, Loyalty Vital in '94 Is a Problem Now," *New York Times*, Oct. 17, 1996, p. B8.

5. Al From quoted in Michael Kelly, "You Say You Want a Revolution," *New Yorker*, Nov. 21, 1994, p. 58.

6. R. W. Apple, Jr., "A Deflated Presidency," *New York Times*, Jan. 25, 1995, p. A15. Joe Klein, "The New Deal," *Newsweek*, Dec. 26, 1994/ Jan. 2, 1995, p. 22. Jack Newfield, "It's Time to Dump Bill Clinton," *New York Post*, Nov. 22, 1994, pp. 1, 16. Ted Van Dyck quoted in Kelly, "You Say You Want a Revolution," p. 65.

7. Richard L. Berke, "Polls Finds Public Doubts Key Parts of G.O.P.'s Agenda," *New York Times*, Feb. 28, 1995, p. A21. Bill Clinton, State of the Union Address, Jan. 24, 1995.

8. Bob Woodward, *The Choice* (New York: Simon and Schuster, 1996), p. 139.

9. Remarks by the president to the National League of Cities, Mar. 13, 1995.

10. Remarks by the president to the American Society of Newspaper Editors, Apr. 7, 1995.

11. Remarks by the president at fiftieth anniversary commemorative ceremonies remembering Franklin D. Roosevelt, Apr. 12, 1995.

12. Bill Clinton, address to the nation on administration budget proposal, June 13, 1995. Dan Balz and Richard Morin, "Public Agrees with Goals of the GOP," *Washington Post*, Jan. 6, 1995, p. A1. William Schneider, "Putting the 'Clint' in Clinton," *Washington Post*, May 28, 1995, p. C1. "Clinton Gains on Dole," *Rocky Mountain News*, July 27, 1995, p. 45A. Apple, "A Deflated Presidency," p. A1. Mark J. Penn and Douglas E. Schoen, "Why Our Game Plan Worked," *Time*, Fall 1996, p. 79.

13. Mary Matalin quoted in Ann Devroy, "Opponents' Issues Drive Clinton's Recovery," *Washington Post*, Oct. 9, 1995, p. A14.

14. Woodward, *The Choice*, pp. 237–38. Alison Mitchell, "Stung by Defeats in '94, Clinton Regrouped and Co-opted G.O.P. Strategies," *New York Times*, Nov. 7, 1995, pp. B1, B5.

15. Adam Clymer, "Battle over the Budget," *New York Times*, Oct. 27, 1995, p. D21. Woodward, *The Choice*, pp. 312–13.

16. Clymer, "Battle over the Budget," p. D21. Doyle McManus, "Clinton Coming out on Top in Budget Tussle," *Los Angeles Times*, Nov. 16, 1995, pp. A1, A23. Bill Kristol quoted in Jacob Weisberg, "Fear and Self-Loathing," *New York*, Aug. 19, 1996, p. 35.

17. Todd S. Purdum, "As Long Promised, President Vetoes G.O.P. Budget," *New York Times*, Dec. 7, 1995, pp. A1, B15. Elizabeth Drew, *Showdown* (New York: Simon and Schuster, 1996), p. 323. Richard L. Berke, "Clinton Ratings over 50% in Poll as G.O.P. Declines," *New York Times*, Dec. 14, 1995, pp. A1, B17.

18. Alison Mitchell, "Clinton Campaign Finds Harmony after Swift Exit by Morris," *New York Times*, Oct. 15, 1996, p. A25.

19. Bill Clinton, State of the Union Address, Jan. 23, 1996.

20. Bob Dole, "The Future and the Values That Will Shape It," Jan. 23, 1996.

21. Pat Buchanan and Phil Gramm quoted in Kevin Merida, "Friends, Foes Fault Dole's Performance," *Washington Post*, Jan. 25, 1996, p. A1.

22. Adam Clymer, "Republicans Told to Brace for Vote on Minimum Wage," *New York Times*, Apr. 18, 1996, pp. A1, B6. Adam Clymer, "Senate Passes Health Bill with Job-to-Job Coverage," *New York Times*, Apr. 24, 1996, pp. A1, B6. Todd S. Purdum, "Clinton Proposes U.S. Tax Credits for College Aid," *New York Times*, June 5, 1996, pp. A1, B6.

23. Bill Clinton, opening remarks by the president in roundtable discussion on school uniform program, Feb. 24, 1996. Tim Poor, "High Court's Concerns Spur Hearing on Death-Row Law," *St. Louis Post-Dispatch*, June 4, 1996, p. A1. Lee Rennert, "Clinton Signs Molester-Notification Bill," *Sacramento Bee*, May 18, 1996, p. A5. Melissa Healy, "Clinton Signals He'd Sign Anti–Gay Marriage Bill," *Los Angeles Times*, May 23,

1996, p. A15. Bill Clinton, remarks at Women's International Convention of God in Christ, May 30, 1996.

24. Robert Kuttner, "Thinking Small," *Washington Post*, Sept. 10, 1996, p. A15. Dan Balz and David S. Broder, "Dole Team Seeks to Seize Fall Agenda," *Washington Post*, Apr. 14, 1996, p. A1. Richard L. Berke, "Clinton Lead Is Unaffected by Troubles," *New York Times*, June 26, 1996, p. A14. Robert Pear, "Clinton to Sign Welfare Bill," *New York Times*, Aug. 1, 1996, pp. A1, A22.

25. Adam Nagourney, "Dole Portrays Clinton As Misguided," *New York Times*, June 26, 1996, p. A14. Adam Clymer, "House Approves Repealing of Ban on Assault Guns," *New York Times*, Mar. 23, 1996, p. A1. Richard L. Berke, "Dole Sends Message of Inclusion to Abortion-Rights Republicans," *New York Times*, July 22, 1996, pp. A1, A12. Katharine Q. Seelye, "Dole Repeats His Doubts That Tobacco Is Addictive," *New York Times*, June 29, 1996, p. 7.

26. Katharine Q. Seelye, "Dole Offers Economic Plan Calling for Broad Tax Cut," *New York Times*, Aug. 6, 1996, pp. A1, A13. "The Hail-Mary Tax Play," *New York Times*, Aug. 4, 1996, sec. 4, p. 14. Dan Balz, "Bold Tax Proposal, Populism Could Be Risky Business," *Washington Post*, Aug. 6, 1996, p. A6.

27. Howard Kurtz, "As Vote Nears, Americans Tuning Out Campaign '96." *Washington Post*, Oct. 10, 1996, p. A1.

28. Garry Wills, "Hating Hillary," *New York Review of Books*, Nov. 14, 1996, p. 12.

29. Bob Dole, Republican party acceptance speech, Aug. 15, 1996. Bob Dole quoted in Rachel L. Swarns, "Dole Is Spirited and Hopes It's Catching," *New York Times*, Nov. 4, 1996, p. A1.

30. Bob Dole on Clinton as liberal quoted in Edward Walsh, "Dole's New Battle Cry," *Washington Post*, Sept. 29, 1996, p. A12. Bob Dole on Dick Morris quoted in David Maraniss and Peter Baker, "Clinton's Top Political Adviser Quits," *Washington Post*, Aug. 30, 1996, p. A39.

31. Transcript of the second presidential debate, Oct. 17, 1996. *New York Times*/CBS poll in Richard L. Berke, "Aggressive Turn by Dole Appears to Be Backfiring," *New York Times*, Oct. 22, 1996, p. A1. Bob Dole quotes from Adam Nagourney, "Dole Unleashes His Tough Talk on Immigration," *New York Times*, Oct. 18, 1996, pp. A1, A27; Adam Nagourney, "Dole Sees Failure of Three Decades of Anti-Bias Fight," *New York Times*, Oct. 29, 1996, pp. A1, A21; Katharine Q. Seelye, "Dole Is Imploring Voters to Rise Up Against the Press," *New York Times*, Oct. 26, 1996, p. A1; Eric Planin, "Dole Slams Clinton, the 'Liberal' Media," *Washington Post*, Oct. 25, 1996, p. A1.

32. Remarks of President Clinton at rally, St. Louis, Missouri, Sept. 10,

1996. Todd S. Purdum, "Clinton Co-opts Crime Issues," *New York Times,* Oct. 27, 1996, sec. 1, p. 28. Alison Mitchell, "Clinton Proposes Drug-Testing Plan for Young People," *New York Times,* Oct. 20, 1996, sec. 1, p. 1. Todd S. Purdum, "Gay Groups Attack Clinton on Midnight Signing," *New York Times,* Sept. 22, 1996, sec. 1, p. 22. Howard Kurtz, "Ad on Christian Radio Touts Clinton's Conservative Stands," *Washington Post,* Oct. 15, 1996, p. A9.

33. Alison Mitchell, "Two Clinton Aides Resign to Protest New Welfare Law," *New York Times,* Sept. 12, 1996, pp. A1, B10. Peter Baker and Edward Walsh, "Results Could Give Democratic Centrists Advantage in Future," *Washington Post,* Nov. 7, 1996, pp. A23, A25.

34. Bill Clinton quoted in John F. Harris and Al Kamen, "Victorious Clinton Returns to Face Cabinet Changes," *Washington Post,* Nov. 7, 1996, p. A1. Martin Walker, *The President We Deserve: Bill Clinton, His Rise, Falls, and Comebacks* (New York: Crown Books, 1996), pp. 332–51.

35. Newt Gingrich quoted in Michael Kelly, "Newt's Rage," *New Yorker,* Oct. 7, 1996, p. 42. Dinesh D'Souza quoted in Weisberg, "Fear and Self-Loathing," p. 34.

36. Barbara Vobejda, "Just under Half of Possible Voters Went to the Polls," *Washington Post,* Nov. 7, 1996, p. A30. Jonathan Alter, "Washington Washes Its Hands," *Newsweek,* Aug. 12, 1996, p. 42.

Epilogue: Looking Backward

1. Edward Bellamy, *Looking Backward, 2000–1887* (Boston: Houghton Mifflin, 1926), p. 57. Alan Trachtenberg, *The Incorporation of America* (New York: Hill and Wang, 1982), pp. 49–50.

2. See Janet Maslin, "Film Festival Review," *New York Times,* Oct. 6, 1995, p. C20.

3. See Terrence Rafferty, "Lost at Sea," *New Yorker,* Aug. 7, 1995, pp. 83–85.

4. Robert D. Kaplan, "The Coming Anarchy," *Atlantic Monthly,* Feb. 1994, pp. 46–47. Robert D. Kaplan, *The Ends of the Earth: A Journey at the Dawn of the 21st Century* (New York: Random House 1996), p. 437.

5. Paul Kennedy, "Doomsterism," *New York Review of Books,* Sept. 19, 1996, p. 20. Bill Clinton quoted in *Boston Globe,* July 20, 1994, p. 6. Samuel P. Huntington, "The Clash of Civilizations?" *Foreign Affairs,* Summer 1993, pp. 22–49. Samuel P. Huntington, *The Clash of Civilizations and the Remaking of World Order* (New York: Simon and Schuster, 1996). Edward Luttwak, "Why Fascism Is the Wave of the Future," *London Review of Books,* Nov. 1995, pp. 6–7.

6. Kate Klise, "The New Civil War: Young and Old Square Off in a Battle

over Benefits," *St. Louis Post-Dispatch*, Apr. 14, 1993, p. 1F. Lester C. Thurow, *The Future of Capitalism* (New York: William Morrow, 1996), pp. 96–97. Henry J. Aaron, "The Myths of the Social Security Crisis," *Washington Post*, July 21, 1996, p. C1. Susan Levine, "Aging Baby Boomers Pose Challenge," *Washington Post*, May 21, 1996, p. A9. Jessica Matthews, "The Coming Retirement Crash," *Washington Post*, Jan. 7, 1996, p. C7. Matthew Miller, "Uh-Oh," *New Republic*, Apr. 15, 1996, p. 22.

7. Franklin Roosevelt quoted in Miller, "Uh-Oh," p. 22.

8. Sherryl Henderson, "Youthful Protestors Target Retirees' Lobby," *Gannett News Service*, Feb. 16, 1993.

9. Rob Nelson and Jon Cowan, "An Appeal to Grandma and Grandpa," *Chicago Tribune*, May 8, 1993, p. N21.

10. Peter G. Peterson, *Will America Grow Up Before It Grows Old?* (New York: Random House, 1996), p. 15. Christopher Georges, "The Boring Twenties," *Washington Post*, Sept. 12, 1993, p. C1. Elizabeth Cohen, "On Campus with Eric Liu," *New York Times*, Sept. 15, 1994, p. C1. Matthews, "The Coming Retirement Crash," p. C7. Senator Bob Kerrey quoted in Miller, "Uh-Oh," p. 22. Richard M. Suzman quoted in Levine, "Aging Baby Boomers Pose Challenge," p. A9. Interview with Richard Thau, executive director of Third Millennium, Sept. 30, 1996.

11. Lester C. Thurow, "The Birth of a Revolutionary Class," *New York Times Magazine*, May 19, 1996, pp. 46–47.

12. Edward Bellamy, *Looking Backward*, pp. 323–30.

13. Michael Lind, *The Next American Nation* (New York: Free Press, 1995), pp. 219–33. John Winthrop, "A Model of Christian Charity," in Perry Miller, ed., *The Puritans* (Garden City, N.Y.: Doubleday Anchor, 1956), pp. 79–83. Robert G. Putnam, "Bowling Alone: America's Declining Social Capital," *Journal of Democracy*, Jan. 1995, p. 68. Gary Belsky, "Escape from America," *Money*, July 1994, p. 60.

14. Putnam, "Bowling Alone," pp. 66–73. Timothy Egan, "Many Seeking Security in Private Communities," *New York Times*, Sept. 3, 1995, sec. 1, pp. 1, 22. Edmund J. Blakely and Mary Gail Snyder, *Fortress America: Gates and Walled Communities in the United States* (Cambridge, Mass.: Lincoln Institute of Land Policy, 1995), p. 18. David Guyerson, "No Place Like Home," *Harper's*, Nov. 1992, pp. 55–64. John Wildermuth, "The Dream Dies Hard in L.A.," *San Francisco Chronicle*, Oct. 12, 1995, p. A1. Thurow, *Future of Capitalism*, pp. 264–65.

15. Edward Bellamy quoted in John L. Thomas, *Alternative America: Henry George, Edward Bellamy, Henry Demarest Lloyd, and the Adversary Tradition* (Cambridge: Harvard University Press, 1983), p. 260.

16. Irving Howe, "Two Cheers for Utopia," *Dissent*, Spring 1993, pp. 131–33.

Index